THE FABRIC OF THE WORLD

By the same author:

New Renaissance
Journey into the Eye of a Needle

Henry Moore's sculpture — *Two-piece reclining figure, No. 1* — could serve as a metaphor for this book. The dualism of Self and the world is dissolved in this piece, and the human form is mingled indistinguishably with the rocky substance of the Earth. Myth is present in a hint of the shaft of Zeus coupling with Leda. The sculpture is in two parts (it was the first time Moore had divided the figure) but these are so interdependent that the unity of the whole would be lost if the space between them were varied by a hair's breadth. The sculptor's own favourite siting of this ambiguous work was one remote from habitation, on a moor in Scotland.

I recall the suppressed excitement, such as I'd never encountered in him before, when Moore unexpectedly called on me (we were neighbours at the time) to announce he had just completed something special. For him, it was a breakthrough, and he had to share this with someone. For myself it has become an example of how in our culture the role of oracle often falls to the artist. It happened thirty years before I wrote this book. *M.A.*

THE FABRIC
OF THE WORLD

Towards a Philosophy
of Environment

Maurice Ash

A RESURGENCE BOOK

A Resurgence Book
First published in 1992 by
Green Books
Ford House, Hartland
Bideford, Devon EX39 6EE

© Green Books 1992

Composed in 11 on 13½ pt
New Century Schoolbook by
Chris Fayers, Soldon, Devon EX22 7PF

Printed by Biddles Ltd, Guildford, Surrey

British Library Cataloguing in Publication Data
Ash, Maurice
The Fabric of the World:
Towards a Philosophy of Environment.
I. Title
333.7

ISBN 1-870098-42-0

CONTENTS

Acknowledgements

This book would not have been achieved without the encouragement of Satish Kumar; the corrections and clarifications insisted on by John Elford; and the commitment of Mary Bride Nicholson, who, scorning the modern technology that removes one further and further from the struggle for words, typed and re-typed innumerable versions of what I wrote. I am indebted to them all.

Introduction

THIS WORK is about the meaning of environment. By this I do not refer to what the dictionary says about environment, but to why the meaning of the word has nowadays become so important. This importance will not pass away (though there are some who wish it might), and this is not because our environment will always be with us. What will not go away, rather, is the part environment must henceforth play in making sense of our existence on the earth.

This part, it is becoming ever more evident, challenges in depth the structures by which we now live—and this is why there are those who wish our concern for environment might prove a passing fad. This development is happening at a time, indeed, when it had seemed materialism was set to triumph over all opposition and science was but a short step away from penetrating the mind of God. Just when it had begun to seem we could with impunity exploit the earth indefinitely, environmental concerns have arisen that threaten to overwhelm humankind and, as with global warming, themselves are the product of this knowledge.

Moreover, this phenomenon of environment cannot be compressed into the temple unique to our kind of world, the laboratory; for, if an environment is abstracted for analysis, measurement and treatment, what then takes its place but another environment? And without our temple we are pathetically exposed, even lost: that is the measure of our dependence on measurement. Indeed it is, one understands, the very artificiality of the laboratory that lies at the root of Quantum Theory.

Palpably, then, the soil is being prepared for a new comprehension, perhaps a new vision, of the world. But the danger is that this vision will be betrayed: a danger, not so much to the vision, as for the survival of us all. This betrayal stems from two sources: first, those too uncritical of the vision; and second, those who only want to pervert it. The former are the New Age people; they are the shamans, the bringers of magic. (There is nothing contemptible about this description. Christianity itself— from the Annunciation to the Ascension, with just about everything in that story that happened in between—was classically shamanistic in its origins, and it is not therefore to be despised.)

The second group are those who would make the new paradigm serve the old order—as, of course, the Romans did in absorbing Christianity. These are the greater danger, for our world can no more survive without radical change than could the Roman. The problematic of Green politics, for instance, is symptomatic of this group's perplexities. Both groups, however, disseminate their different illusions, and the priority now is not so much to proclaim the new as to rescue it from its proponents.

To do this I think it is necessary to take a deeper look at our roots than is often associated with a concern for environment. The general superficiality of that concern leaves too many hostages to fortune. Protecting the environment, for instance—or, even worse, managing it—is becoming but a euphemism for serving one set of interests at the expense of another and of doing so by reference to a supposedly ideal state of affairs, perhaps some kind of 'steady state'. Moreover such management assumes—for example, by digging holes to bury our detritus—that it would itself somehow be (excuse the word) a-environmental. Environment is thus in danger

8

of becoming just a continuation of the paradisiacal tradition: a harmonious state of affairs where all conflicts are resolved—according to some omnipotent voice.

This book, then, stems directly from a pamphlet, 'Meanings of Environment', published by *Resurgence* magazine in June 1991; and that pamphlet was itself the product of a series of articles in that magazine over the preceding years. This being so, however, I have to ask why I should be repeating myself: and by what right is even one more tree to be cut down to make this book, or one word added to the spate of published words in which the world is already sinking? After all, others might in time hopefully come to the same sort of conclusions I have reached (or perhaps have already done so), for these are really written in the facts. Nor do I feel any urge to publish because time is short—though it is, and that was what lay behind my hurried earlier publications—for I doubt if anything I say will make any measurable difference to events. Nevertheless, I have been involved now for upwards of two decades in what is commonly called the new paradigm— both in thinking about it and putting thoughts into practice—and I have debts to repay for the richness life has brought me in that respect. If my conclusions are not mainstream in that swelling flood, I can only ask indulgence. Think but

That I have shot mine arrow o'er the house
And hurt my brother.

Above all, however, my justification is that I want to offer a gift to whoever will receive it, because I think I have something to impart. And this is why I do not think I am just repeating myself, for (though anyone would have a right to feel incredulous) the curious thing is that I think I myself now understand what I have been saying all these years in search of the hidden agenda of the Green movement.

Perhaps, however, this is not so very curious. Our intuitions are one kind of understanding, and are just as valid as the arduous arguments with which we must clothe them if we are to share them with others. Be all that as it may, a serious difficulty nevertheless stands in the way of sharing my new-found understanding. We have lost the language in which our forebears made sense of what we call environment. This was the language of myth. Myths, with all their teeming deities, peopled the regions we now characterise by environment: their disappearance has left us at best merely incurious about those regions, at worst denying their existence. From time to time since the Enlightenment befell us attempts have been made—Blake and Yeats come to mind—to fabricate new myths, but these are noble failures which only serve to emphasise our irreparable loss. (Modern psychiatry also invokes ancient myths, but, alas, less to serve the shared spaces of our world than to succour our private lives.)

Certainly it is not the purpose of what follows to re-mythologise environment. The language to do this no longer exists—though it might yet emerge, perhaps through science fiction. We are burdened with the language in which our present-day culture conducts its conversation: a language, as it were, pivoted on the atom, on the substance to which we have supposed the world is reducible. But if the language of shadows and shapes, of waking dreams, is no longer ours, the spaces they filled are still there all round us. To acknowledge this is all that matters—and perhaps, indeed, it were better if those spaces were not filled again.

To approach these matters with only the metaphors of positivism at our disposal is, however, an unavoidable handicap. What can be done, none the less, is to avoid forcing the discussion into some rigidly sequential order of argument, an order such as inheres in the logic of this inadequate language of ours. The language of interdependence, after all, can hardly be the same as that of causation. Hence the writing of what follows will have to be largely alleatoric, and may even seem inconsequential or lapse into repetition. But at least it will be short.

Chapter One

The two sides of one coin

PARADOXICAL THOUGH IT MAY APPEAR, there is one unchallengable starting-point for a discussion of something as pervasive as environment: namely, the dimensionless point that is the alpha and omega of our Western mentality and culture—that is to say, the Self. The Self, as Descartes persuaded us, is the knower of the known—and, vide Bacon, knowledge itself is power. In this possessive society of ours, power over what lies around us is the key to survival. Indeed, things as such are the things they are—separate each from the other, objects known by name and number—the better to be possessed by the Self. Our mastery of the world, then, suggests that the knowledge we have of our environment should derive from the same source: that is, from what the Self observes of it.

And yet... to conceptualise a thing, to define it, is as much as to abstract it from its environment. This act of possession by the Self involves the detachment from their environment of both it and the conceived object: which is as much as to say that environment cannot be abstracted from environment; and furthermore that environment must annihilate Self, which cannot conceive of it. It was, after all, terror at the Self's utter detachment from all surrounding it, its cosmic loneliness, that led Descartes to assert 'God would not deceive us' about the measurements he (Descartes) would have us make, the very knowledge we might have, of the contents of the world from which logically the Self is separate.

Measurement and the quantitative have thus come to be sanctified as a kind of hallowed thread between the Self and the world. Yet there is none the less a certain aridity about the quantitative world we have contrived for ourselves to live in—this mere extension—that bespeaks an impoverishment beyond measure. And, if there is that about the measurable that seems sterile, it is perhaps because before anything can be measured it has to be detached from its surroundings, to lose the dimension of its environment. Or, perhaps, it is because actually God might deceive us. Or both of these.

Automatically, none the less, it is in terms of the Self and what is apart from it, 'out there', that we have sought to comprehend this phenomenon of 'the Environment' that is forcing itself upon our attention. The immediate consequence has been a degradation of the concept. Environment becomes, like everything else 'out there', something to be possessed. Consider, for instance, the Green Belt, which, almost unbelievably, is now commonly taken to be a manifestation of the Environment. It is commonplace for discussion to assume the Green Belt is an environmental issue. As such, it is defended with a fierce moral fervour. Or it is so by some; by others it is coveted for their own uses. And are the defenders of this land any more motivated by high principle than are those who would use it for themselves? Hardly so! For the Green Belt has become a prime symbol of NIMBY (Not In My Backyard) environmentalists. These are those, broadly speaking, who would keep the countryside for themselves—even if, in the course of its being preserved, it would change its character entirely.

The irony is, of course, that originally there was a practical purpose for the Green Belt. This was to stop the town spreading, not just in order to retain the town's identity, but precisely so that the countryside might be the better urbanised. (In practice, in fact, Green Belts have been rightly criticised for their nondescript character.) There are indeed still those who adhere to this original orthodoxy of the Green Belt, although it has largely been rendered obsolete by the changing form of cities: that is, from being single- to many-centred. (And there is a whole new psychic experience there.) Whether right or wrong, however, these urban romantics do not constitute the real antinomy of Nimbyism. That distinction is reserved for those whose political constituency lies within the old cities and who would endorse the Green Belt to retain their supporters within it, squeezing the population upwards into high-rise and high-density public housing—all in pursuit of an ideal of 'urbanity'. And so the unholy conspiracy to sacrifice our cities on the altar of a perversion of 'environment' is allowed to proceed.

This can happen because environment has been reified: turned into a thing. It is likewise by this means that the notion of the Environment, as a generalisation of all and sundry particular environments, has been conjured up. 'The Environment' is, in fact, simply a metaphysical construct; its plausibility as a substantive entity is conferred solely by its apartness from the Self. A consequence of these claims to recognition is evident in the case of the so-called 'greenhouse effect'.

By characterising the earth's atmosphere as a greenhouse and then equating this with the environment, the stage is set for political and economic negotiations—whether national or international, concerning differential fiscal charges on fuels, say, or sophisticated 'pollution swaps' between nations—focussed on the presumed causal agents of the warming of this 'thing'. These negotiations must be complicated enough, not least because as the greenhouse effect develops it may favour (or disfavour) some parts of the earth more than others. (In one scenario, after all, the Sahara may flower again whilst all the Mediterranean regions of the Northern hemisphere become desert and many great cities drown.) Over and above this relativism there is the question of how the Third World— let alone the Second—is to be persuaded not to follow the profligate energy path to growth of the First. How are we to prevent the world's deprived nations from exacting the so symbolic revenge—a redressment of the world's social balance through global warming—they may glimpse as consequent on this course of action? By bribing them, perhaps, to practise only Alternative Technology? They would be saints to agree to quash their envy in this way.

These problematic negotiations to control the green-house effect rest, in fact, on a chimera: on a transmutation of the earth's atmosphere into the metaphysic of 'the Environment'. By this sleight of thought the Environment is converted into a something 'out there': something monolithic and fully intelligible to us, susceptible to rational control. This notion of the Environment is therefore a confirmation of the idea of reality that underlies all our exploitation of matter, just as it equally confirms the exploiting Self. Now it will surely be said that the agents of global warming—the burning of fossil fuels, whether in power stations or motor cars, etc.—are real enough; yet, without raising the question of, say, how real are the atoms of which a motor car is composed, it must be pointed out that this notion of reality does no more than employ the categories of thought to which we are accustomed. A motorcar, no doubt, is a motor car, is a motor car; but it is a motor car only in any one of innumerably different situations, in each one of which it is arguably a different thing—just as the Eskimos reputedly have some twenty different words for what we call 'snow': or, conversely, as the Japanese have no word for 'I' out of context.

The consequence of our fixation on the categories of an assumed reality, then, is a concentration upon the multifarious users, as users, of fossil fuels, whom we hold responsible for environmental changes, with all the unresolvable complexities of power that must ensue therefrom. If we are seriously concerned about global warming we would, perhaps, be better advised to cut off, or regulate, the supplies of fossil fuels at source. A prerequisite for doing this, however, would be to talk in terms of the earth's atmosphere, rather than of the Environment, for then there would be no illusion that some ideal solution, some rational apportionment of energy consumption, might exist. This more modest frame of reference is necessary because, conversely, 'the Environment' would seem to imply all that is knowable about the world we inhabit and which hence empowers all our values.

None of this should be taken to suggest that science cannot help us with what we like to call our environmental problems; only that we should realise the limitations of that help. For, to look at the matter conversely, rather than owing the greenhouse effect to the achievements of science, we owe it to science's inherent deficiencies. For, had science been able to foresee the greenhouse effects of the internal combustion engine, say, it is surely unlikely that our forefathers would have launched into its manufacture, or have taken on trust the notion of knowledge underlying it. But had science had such prescience, it could not have invented the internal combustion engine, for that invention hinged upon the patently unreal isolation from their environments of manifold forces and substances, the discovery of which by this dubious process eventually led to the invention in question.

To come down to earth, so to speak, consider pollution of the air we breathe. The word 'pollution' is of course pejorative. In Christian—that is St. Augustine's—thought, it is a 'perversion' of God's natural order, and hence redolent of evil. It betokens an immoral state of affairs, a crime against 'the Environment'. There is always a cost in rectifying any human failing: in this case, for scrubbing the chimneys of coal-fired power stations (and somehow disposing of the sludge), or raising the costs of fuel by fiscal means, or just for buying the masks children in Los Angeles, Tokyo or Athens wear on their way to school—there, no doubt, to acquire the very knowledge that has polluted the air they breathe. Pollution thus becomes a factor in the cash nexus, in which it will compete with all the other objects calling for the Self's attention. And so one could go on, showing how most, if not all, talk of the Environment is one side of a coin of which the other is the Self. The case of destruction of the rain forests, for instance, comes to mind. The irony in this case could not be more striking. We admonish the Brazilians and others from the position of benefit we have reached by the comparable actions of our ancestors, between four and six thousand years ago, in deforesting the land to convert it into pasture. It is a position that is all too obviously self-righteous.

One might say, then, that environment has no sooner been discovered than it has been abused. Environment itself has been contaminated; and, given our ruling paradigm of thought—centred as it is on the Self—this contamination was perhaps unavoidable. That such a degeneration of meaning should so soon have occurred—even threatening to discredit out concern over our own destruction—is but symtomatic of the problem. I do not imply by this that the definition of any word, even 'environment', can be fixed. That would be to think in terms of the essences of things, which would be to resort to idealism as a means of evading the dualism—of subject and object, of Self and the world—that bewitches us now. To take this road (as many unquestioningly have done) would be to submerge the notion of environment in the general decadence of these times. Any ideal is fixed and allows of no conversation. But environment is too crucial a notion to be lost in this way. It lies at the core of the new paradigm (acceptance of which is now virtually a commonplace) that must displace the Cartesian one of rational idealism by which our lives have hitherto been ruled. It is therefore crucial to prevent the notion of environment being shaped— as it is in such danger of being shaped—by the Self, and to explore its meaning in a new context of experience.

Chapter Two

Concerning the Self

IT WOULD BE AS WELL, then, to be clear what is this Self of which we need to be disembarrassed. Has anyone ever sensed—touched, seen or smelt—this Self? Is it one's body, the most obviously constant material factor of one's life? But this, unlike the Self, is in perpetual material flux; not one molecule of which it is now composed will be contained in it in—what is it?—six months' time. (Small compensation, that maybe once or twice in your lifetime you might harbour a molecule previously a part of Jesus Christ. At least, this would be a very catholic Self.) Or is the Self just a unique sum of memories? Just a box of electronic tricks, then? Or am I what you are not—and you and you and everything else in the universe? Perhaps this is getting nearer to it—though only by saying what I am not. Yet, ultimately, this is tantamount to saying I am what my environment is not—and what is my environment? So am I just what I think I am? But if so, what is thought? An activity of the brain, no doubt. But am 'I' only my brain? Are not other parts of me just as important, just as much me? An activity of the mind, then? Perhaps we're getting there at last. But has anyone ever touched this mind? All in all, in fact, what is it but an invention, a fabrication having the property of allowing the Self separately to exist? Which brings us back to where we started.

Of course questions like this, and many other and more sophisticated ones, are nothing new. They simply assume the substantive nature of the Self. More profit may be had from considering the uses the notion of Self has served through history. This can largely be traced in the thoughts of all the great—and the less great—philosophers, for arguably the concept of Self is central to Western thought. However, saying this is not necessarily to subscribe to the intellectual arrogance—so prevalent since Plato, at least—that all else will follow if only our philosophy is right in theory. Much misery could be ascribed to that notion; and anyway it is arguable, not just that the philosophy of any period is only a rationalisation of its culture, but further that the arrogance of the idea in question is but a function of the centrality of the Self in Western civilisation. Nevertheless, philosophy is surely at least something of a guide to how the wind has blown, and is blowing; and the Self has been its creature.

To speculate, then, whence the concept of Self stemmed, one could do worse than begin with the development of literacy. Literacy is surely a great aid to privacy, to withdrawal from the immediacy of everyday life, a process noticeable in Western society from the late Middle Ages. That which thus withdraws, whether the writer or the reader, has a quasi-tangible presence. Moreover, literacy more or less fixes the meaning of words: that is, it determines things, makes objects out of all the flux of speech—though this fixity in an ever-changing world threatens us with perpetual disillusionment. (There is the case of the collector of Celtic tales whose subject arrived back on his doorstep in the morning, having walked ten miles home and back, saying 'You'll not be writing down what I told you last night, will you?' To fix his words on paper, that is to say, would have taken the life from them, depriving them of context, of their environment.) And to make objects is to make subjects; it is to fix the mode of dualistic thought in which the 'I' is crucial.

Presumably, in addition, literacy is an all but indispensible instrument for encapsulating the Self in the continuity of a story—for this is what has been held to be an essential condition for the implantation of the notion of Self: the telling of stories. And so it may be—although, significantly, the notion of Self is seemingly not to be found in Homer. But, even if so, what a patent contrivance is the concept of a story! Real life scarcely knows such continuities, let alone those banal contrivances of the hero and the villain, etc.

It is perhaps the abiding attraction for us of the Homeric Greeks, prior to the corruption of their civilisation in the Classic period, that for them the Self was not yet substantiated, that the gods bestowed no immortality on any man—their own permanence, indeed, being in some doubt. In our eyes, this lends a certain spontaneity and freshness to the people of that culture, a non-dualism signalled by the nakedness of their games and festivals. This could hardly be said, however, of that other great tributary of our civilisation, the Judaic. It was in self-consciousness that Adam and Eve saw they were naked. In eating of the Tree of Knowledge of good and evil—those primal opposites—they became each the knower: each the knower of a Self made patent by the un-Selflike behaviour of (in St. Augustine's phrase) 'our disobedient member'. We, of course, take for granted that we are clothed; it attracts no philosophical attention (that is, if Hamlet doesn't count as philosophy), despite its origins in such knowledge. Yet clothes are the carapace, together with a name, which enables the Self both to objectify the world and to fashion its own reality. The language of clothing, in fact, only serves to conceal our actual incommens-urability—and, of course, to confirm our species identity. Any philosophy of clothing, surely, would be all about power: about power and Self.

In this light it is not too wild a suggestion that the mystifying practice of circumcision (and not only the Jewish form of it, of course, though in Genesis it follows quite closely on the heels of the discovery by Adam and Eve of their special knowledge) arose from a consciousness of the Self. Let us remember, after all, that Christianity has its roots in Judaism, and circumcision is the core of Judaism. To expose to God that most private and important part of his body is to have a man recognise that between the world and himself as a unique being a compact, marked by sacrifice, must exist. In Genesis, of course, this is presented as the mark of belonging to a tribe, the one that alone could hear the word of God; but to posit such a tribe is as much as to make a claim for the autonomy, the selfhood, of each of its members. This is the very kernel of dualism.

In Christianity, St. Paul gave exemption from circumcision, speaking instead of the circumcision of the heart. (Until about a hundred years ago, indeed, the practice was virtually unknown, if not anathematised as unnatural, in the West; the medical priesthood, with a wave of conversions a hundred years ago, somewhat altered that.) However it was not so much adherence to the Law as an act of faith that was demanded of Christians. Yet, except in appearance, this did not mean a reversion to the non-dualism of Ancient Greece. (I am not suggesting [quite] that anyone not circumcised is non-dualistic in their mentality!) That pass had already been sold to Christianity by the neo-Platonists. Faith was, to be sure, found in Nature rather than Man (originating as it did in the Garden: for as St. Augustine said, 'Evil is contrary to Nature'); but, since it was not the tribe that was henceforth to be distinguished but the whole of mankind that was to be saved, no special bodily mark would have been appropriate to Christians. Nevertheless, the Judaic duality is deeply ingrained in us. St. Augustine's expression of it still serves: 'The earthly city was created by self-love reaching the point of contempt for God, the Heavenly City by the love of god carried as far as contempt of self.'

It was Plato (in the Phaedrus) who made the crucial distillation of the soul out of dualistic thought. (It had, to be sure, always been latent in the Orphic myth.) The soul henceforth conveyed the Self; and it is because Plato's thought-system is marked by the establishment at its centre of the Self that it remains all too intelligible to us. The concomitant of this establishment of the Self is an ontology, a notion of reality, in atomistic terms: in terms of the world as substance. For if the knower is detached from the world, rather than implicate in it, his relationship to it will be as is subject to object; and though he, the knower, will be constant in space and time, the world will be known to him in all its spatial and temporal parts.

From this it is only a step to the process of reification: of making things with words where otherwise nothing is. And this is pertinent, not just to metaphysics—to fabricating things of which the senses have no experience (like the soul)—but also to the very premise that the world is constituted of substance, a premise which only in our own times has science itself begun to call in doubt. It is likewise only appropriate that philosophy—again in our own times—should increasingly be driven by Wittgenstein's understanding of its task: to struggle against the bewitchment of our intelligence by language.

An atomised world, one constituted of distinct substances, is one in which the interactions between these must give a dominant place to the notion of cause. This in turn implies the premise of a First Cause, and hence also the act of Creation, and therefore of God as the actor: all this is implicit in the notion of Self. Evidently, the premise of a First Cause, which follows from the atomisation of the world—for the concept of the divisibility of substance also presumes its congruence—is conducive to monotheism. It says nothing about what part God should play in the world—and, of course, Jews, Christians and Muslims fatefully chose different solutions to this. But that they should have been in a position to make such claims was because they shared the dualism rooted in the notion of Self and its salvation.

Dualistic thought could be expected to dictate that the Self should be concerned with objects, things as such, whether itself or other objects in the external world. The knower, knowing itself as an object, will identify knowledge with the objects knowledge refers to. What is not discrete and specific will be, if not actually unknowable, then unimportant. In this way environmental considerations, considerations of context, have been of only minor concern in Western culture. That being said, however, Christianity pursued an extreme form of this logical format: namely, by embodying the Self in the notion of the person. That is to say that the person, for Christianity, was autonomous. It was not—as, say, we conceive of the individual—just a part in some social body and therefore subject to its laws; it was rather conceived as responsible, if at all, only to God's laws. This in fact simply reflected Christian withdrawal from the world in the face of the disaster of Rome's decline and fall: its rendering unto God what was God's and to Caesar what was Caesar's. The extreme expression of this other-worldliness, of course, was monasticism, held up as the truest fulfillment of a Christian life. (By contrast, Mohammed declared 'No monkery in Islam'.) In the notion of the person, then, we have an expression of the inwardness (if the use of that metaphor can be allowed to pass) that has been characteristic of the Self in Christian civilisation. This so-called inwardness, in fact, is symptomatic over the centuries and in many cultures of movements such as stoicism, puritanism, etc.

St. Augustine's doctrine of Original Sin—and he and St. Paul, after all, are the real founders of what we call 'Christianity': so to speak, its Abraham—was obviously indicative of the notion of the Self as an autonomous person. It implied that one's salvation (and the Self must needs want to be saved) was to be found elsewhere—an elsewhere we might as well call 'Heaven': not, that is, by one's works on earth (for the person by definition cannot enter into worldly relationships) but only through faith and hence, as a first step, by baptism in the Church. In this sense, at least, the Self in Christendom is not an isolate; mystically it is a member of its community, the Church, and under God part of His natural order. It was through Heaven or Hell, not on earth, that the dualism of the soul manifested itself, whether in bliss or in misery. To this extent those regions were metaphysically to those times as environment is to us: regions the more indistinct the nearer approached, but their postulation nevertheless indispensible for making sense of life on earth. This might at least give pause to the fashionable laying at Christianity's door of all responsibility for the despoliation of the earth. The matter is surely far more complex. One might, for instance, with equal or more justice lay a contrary accusation of other-worldliness at the door of early Christianity. Perhaps the most one should say, without leading to altogether too great a digression, is that a heavy price was bound to be paid in one form or another— and it has been paid in different forms, both Catholic and Protestant—to accommodate the logic of the soul.

At all events it was Christianity that for some one and a half millenia set the mould of Western civilisation. It was with the new paradigm of the Enlightenment in the seventeenth century that this mould was broken: specifically, with Descartes' Cogito. That is, with the pronouncement that the Self was a substance of which the only function was to think. From one perspective, this was a decisive lurch into the essential inwardness of the Self. But from another—and one that does not depend upon the Self having an inner and an outer structure—it was the Self abandoning Heaven, and seeking its salvation on earth. The implication of this quasi-Faustian act was the objectification of the world, the detachment of observer from observed that we now associate with science.

In fact, apart from this implied and all-pervasive attitude, it was less Descartes than Newton who, by getting his results without respect to Descartes' rational idealism, most influenced the Enlightenment. And Newton was secretly an Arian—secretly, because had he not concealed it (as in fact it was concealed for some two and a half centuries) he would have been expelled from his living at Cambridge. That is, Newton disbelieved in the Trinity—that great underpinning of the Church's privileged reconciliation of Heaven and Earth—and subscribed to a virtually Islamic monotheism. (Arius was the loser in the fourth century dispute which determined the direction Christianity should take.) This Arian persuasion of Newton's might be seen as a tell-tale of the way the winds of thought were blowing: away from the authority of religion and towards salvation by works. The Self would address the world—even though, in Descartes' scheme of things, it was the only extensionless point in that world; and there was to be nothing in the world it could not know.

Now I apologise to those readers not deeply interested in the history of ideas, for mostly it is a story of self-deception. They have my sympathy for staying with me thus far—but we are coming to the home stretch of this aspect of this work. That is to say, the history of post-Cartesian thought might be understood as an alternation, a counterpoint, between solipsism, the notion that only the Self is real, and the premise that reality, and particularly social reality, is external: between, say, the Romantic movement of Rousseau and his Noble Savage and Marxism with its Soviet Man, by way of the empiricism of Locke's individualism, Schopenhauer's view that the Self was the microcosm of the world ('The world is my idea'), Kant's 'counter-Copernican revolution', putting the person at the centre of moral space, and Kirkegaard's (and others') Existentialism. All the while, there has been the relentless doctrine of science, making Man as thinker master of the physical world, whilst Freud, seemingly despairing of changing the external world, put at the beginning of his great *The Interpretation of Dreams* Virgil's line: 'If I cannot move heaven, I will stir up the underworld.'

The end of the Cartesian paradigm, then, within which all this dialectic occurred, has been marked by the second half of Wittgenstein's life's work, after he had renounced the solipsism, and all its logic, of the first half—and, of course, by many other contemporary events besides, notably the emergence of Quantum Mechanics, as also, say, by the treatment of the object in Cubism. Significantly, the nub of Wittgenstein's approach—which is precisely not a theory, conventionally understood, but a long catalogue of examples—is a rejection (or perhaps, rather, a ridiculing) of the notion of a substantive Self; and it is prefaced by an (albeit respectful) exposure of the inadequacies of St. Augustine's theory of language, upon which, virtually unnoticed, the whole subsequent edifice has been constructed over the centuries.

It should, however, perhaps be noted that there is a current attempt to use Quantum Mechanics to prove that the Self does substantially exist: that our bodies are 'Bose-Einstein condensates', determined by the characteristic quantum behaviour of certain photon particles—all of which may be true, but nowhere in this theory is there mention of language and of its role in categorising this somewhat ghostly presence as a Self. Likewise, a popular book on science has assured us that in physics we are but one step from knowing 'the mind of God'—but it does not tell us what might happen in the taking of that step, nor about the other parts of God. These examples are only important as serving to show how tenacious the old ways of thought are likely to be in a last-ditch defence of the detritus of the last four centuries. Let Wittgenstein, then, put a contrary view (*Tractatus* 6.371 and 2):

The whole modern conception of the world is founded on the illusion that the so-called laws of nature are the explanation of natural phenomena.

Thus today people stop at the laws of nature, treating them as something inviolable, just as God and Fate were treated in past ages.

And in fact both are right and both wrong: though the view of the ancients is clearer in so far as they have a clear and acknowledged terminus, while the modern system tries to make it look as if *everything* were explained.

This, then, is at least a different, and cautionary, view to the conventional claims of science. Its justification, painfully established in the second half of Wittgenstein's life's work, stems from the premise that the Self is a metaphysical chimera. The root of the matter is that our language cannot be private; it is inextricably intermingled with social behaviour. Words do not define objects, putting labels on them; their meanings lie in their use, in all its kaleidoscopic variety. We, as users of words, are not solitary intelligences, with no other function than to think; we are constituted of our everyday interactions with one another. Moreover, it is as much our feelings as our intellects that compose us—'The heart has its reasons that reason knows not of", said Pascal—and this also is just another questionable duality.

Indeed the distinction between intellect and feeling is one of many dualities ripe for deconstruction. Dogen, the greatest of Zen philosophers, had much to say on this question, back in the thirteenth century. Mind and body cannot be compartmentalised, the one pure, the other impure: there is only 'body-mind', just as the world and the Self are not separate. 'The Way is attained surely with the body.' To exalt the mind at the cost of the body is to achieve a spurious spirituality. We in the West have some catching up to do if this is the case; for the implication is that it is not the isolated Self, seeking its own salvation in self-love, that is the proper given of philosophy, its Cogito, but the everyday forms of life in which all our selves are embedded. It is their context that lends meaning to the objects we speak about, and this clearly points to the significance of environment in our thinking about the world.

Now the foregoing brief review of the centrality of the idea of the Self in Western (and other) thought down the ages is admittedly inadequate by almost any standard. (Nevertheless, one is emboldened in one's speculations by remembering William James' earnest introspection in search of his 'Self of selves', which he located somewhere between the head and the throat.) My purpose, however, was only to suggest that that centrality has indeed obtained. Two further comments remain to be made. First, if it is indeed true that this Self is a metaphysical chimera, then there can be no need to examine its structure, and in particular its inwardness and outwardness and what might mediate between these. There is no substantive body to be explored. This is not to say all such talk should be debarred. Such metaphors no doubt have their uses. But it will be the circumstances of any such use, rather than any Self that uses them, that will merit examination.

Second, it needs to be reiterated that it is in terms of the context of Western thought that we have here been looking at the notion of Self, because nothing could better illustrate the complacent insularity of that thought. In fact, the issue of the Self has been the overt concern of Eastern cultures over thousands of years; and because it has been overt it has been far more rigorously examined there. It could be said, for instance, to have marked the divide between Buddhist and Vedantic civilisations. And yet a recent book of over five hundred pages on the sources of the Self by a respected Western academic philosopher could find space only in a footnote to say that this different tradition apparently existed, but regretted the author could say nothing about it. The encouraging thing is, however, that Wittgenstein—who equally had no awareness of the Eastern tradition, except perhaps indirectly through Schopenhauer—entirely by his own efforts virtually reconstituted the thinking of Nagarjuna, the greatest of the Buddhist philosophers from nearly two thousand years ago. This is the true mark of his significance, just as it is a measure of the distance we ourselves have yet to travel.

Chapter Three

Beyond the mechanistic

IT IS NOT ONLY what Wittgenstein said, but that he said it when he did, that matters. It's true that several decades elapsed—one might put it between the early 1930s and the first Arab oil crisis of 1973—between, on the one hand, the upending in his writings, and even more in his dialogues, of the premises of Western thought and, on the other, widespread public doubts about the course on which our lives are set. But such intervals of time are not uncommon when the greatest changes are afoot; there was, after all, about the same interval (together with the Thirty Years War) between Descartes' 'Method' and the impact of the Enlightenment on the pattern of European life, including eventually the English Revolution of 1688 from which liberal democracy stemmed. In any case, the changes in our ways of life are not coming about by any conscious application of Wittgenstein's ideas, for he never propounded any theory. Though this would hardly be in the nature of those ideas, it might nevertheless happen later—and much the same could be said, for instance, about the impact on our values of the vision given by Quantum Mechanics—but it is, rather, an indefinable unease with the course of events that is bringing all our assumptions into question.

This unease is finding expression ,in the notion of environment. This notion has been paraded to clothe the undisguisable inadequacies of public policy. The British

Department of the Environment, for instance, was established in 1971—and became an instant monstrosity, making up in size what it lacked in meaning. (It was, and is, a prime example of 'solution by institution'.) What was being discovered was that problems were arising to which the given categories of ideas did not apply; cities, in particular, were not keeping to their boundaries. What could be more natural, then, than to seek solutions in a larger scale of actions: in the quantitative, rather than the qualitative! The instinct to treat these problems 'environmentally' was, however, right; but to suppose that something called 'the Environment' was just the manageable sum of those problems was vacuous. The Department of the Environment itself has been, for all to see, nothing but a sorry monument to the flaw in our way of thinking. Can one, after all, departmentalise environment?

But the intuition was right. Our thoughts are indeed flawed, and the idea of environment is a challenge to the core of them. The first aspect of this challenge is to the Cartesian notion that the observer is detached from the observed, a notion which derives from and is sanctioned by the concept of the isolated Self. The second challenge is to the equally Cartesian principle of reductionism. For, having established the inviolate Self, the Cartesian scheme of things has been free to reduce the world to bits and pieces, to atomise it, the better to know and to master it. Indeed, the Self has a duty to itself so to proceed; nothing less could validate its own unique standing here on earth. These, then, are the twin pillars of Cartesianism upon which our lives have been built. And these are what the very notion of environment challenges.

We refer intuitively to environment, perhaps because it immerses us. We are thus not detached from it, nor it from us. And likewise our environment is a totality, essentially indivisible. Should we separate out one part of our environment, we must in so doing engage with it instrumentally, and to us it will then cease to be the environment of our actions and become a component of them. Environment is that which our intentional actions themselves are not. And yet we have no calculus, no rules even, to guide these instincts. The scientific method, which we understand so well, precisely does not apply. Its application is indeed what is making us ill; and like a sick animal that cures itself by seeking a different herbage, we turn away from it. But because all we understand is the possession of things, we are only making ourselves worse. An environment cannot be possessed.

Yet we persist. We try, for instance, to measure environment—the measurement of the extension of things being our means of establishing their material existence. But environment is not a discrete, and hence measurable, object. That whole of which any discrete object is part is not an indivisible one. It is, rather, precisely part of some divisible entity; indeed, it is by its parts, the sum of them, that any such entity articulates its boundaries with the world. That chair over there: it has legs, back and a seat and, each lending meaning to the other, they articulate a 'chair'. But the object thus defined is not an environment or any part of it. Indeed, it has not as yet even an identity— for definition and identity are not the same. The chair's identity comes from what it is not: it is not that other chair, nor that table, etc. Discrete objects are characteristically identified by what they are not; but they could not be what they are not if they were not constituted of their own parts. An environment, conversely, has no finite boundary with the world (which is why an ecosystem, with its man-ordained boundaries, is not an environment); the calculus of extension cannot apply to it. There are no discrete parts of it, and it is indefinable. But it is not therefore inexistent.

Or we persist in our efforts to order our intuitive resort

to the notion of environment by means of the technique of cost-benefit analysis. Economics calls this technique in aid because its conventional market analysis is patently unable to measure 'environmental' factors. Cost-benefit analysis, then, is economics without the Market but as if there were a Market. It tells us what values would be if there were any values, which environmentally there aren't. It is thus clearly an exercise in metaphysics, not to say mystification. Obviously this presents no difficulty to anyone who takes the substantive existence of this mysterious and all-pervasive Market for granted, although it is actually nothing but a stipulation of economic theory. (The Market no more exists than does the Environment.) In the case of this technique's first major practical use— the Third London Airport Inquiry of 1967—cost-benefit analysis (which was allowed to dominate those proceedings) sought to measure, amongst other things, the value of a mediaeval church (this turned out to be its insurance value) and the value of businessmen's time in getting to the various candidate sites. The fact that in the fresh light of day, once outside the claustrophobia of that Inquiry, the results were publicly ridiculed and rejected, has not deterred exponents of cost-benefit analysis from trying again to measure the 'environmental costs' of activities such as precisely are not costed in actual life. The businessman is not to be so lightly discarded in our culture as the model of humanity.

Monetary costs and values are, in fact, a function of the divisibility of goods and services into discrete exchangeable units. Monetary units of measure have no other rationale; they are not somehow mathematically autonomous, with a life of their own. Indeed, to reduce the value of a thing to its monetary worth is to isolate it, to confirm it as a thing; and, in the same way, to judge of an enterprise and its exploitation of resources in terms of some one criterion, that of its profitability, is to isolate it from its environment. Herein lies the power of money: it serves to atomise society. This may help explain why cost-benefit analysis has been termed (borrowing a phrase from John Stuart Mill) 'nonsense on stilts'; it is on stilts because it is superimposed on an edifice—the Marginal Utility theory of Value—that is itself philosophically shaky. It very well illustrates the causal interdependence of the measure and the measured. In brief, it is the metaphysical wonder of the age. What is patently extraordinary is the thrall exercised by measurement—any measurement—over the powers that be, desperate to give credence to such metaphysics. The true cost of this credibility, however, is in the atrophy of words—and the feelings words can explore—and whereby, actually, all qualitative issues can alone be resolved.

Or, again, if not by measurement, we may nevertheless try to concretise environment through traditional communitarian movements such as Communism or Socialism. These are, in fact, products of the other great antidote (the Greek one) to the disintegrative effects of dualistic thought: idealism. Idealism serves to compensate for the fragmentation induced by the separation of knower from known. By the process of idealisation we can transmute the manifold expressions of any one notion into its essence. From Plato to the present day this has been a main weapon in the defensive armoury of the West against its own acceptance of the cruel logic of dualism. As it did with Plato and his 'Republic', it lends itself to an all-inclusive embrace of society—to Utopia, in fact—since the process of determining the essence of anything, the reality behind the appearance, involves finding what is common to its many forms. It is thus resistant to the dissolution of the forms in terms of which life is conducted; yet it is not necessarily resistant to the critical dissection of those forms. Descartes' method, after all, is known as rational idealism.

This is not the place for a detailed critique of idealism. It would be otiose to repeat what has been better done elsewhere. It may be worth saying, however, that it is no wonder that philosophy in general has traditionally let it be thought that it, of all disciplines, holds the key to Truth, without which all the rest would be inept, for the pretensions of idealism have been at the root of Western thought. And nor is it any wonder, given the dualism of idealistic thought—the subjective evaluation of the objective world—that idealism has been so closely associated with the greatest tyrannies. May we be saved, then, from idealisation of the Environment!

All this is only to say, however, that idealism indeed shares with environmentalism a concern for wholeness. Yet this similarity is a mere deception. The wholeness of the ideal is metaphysical. It may conjure some representation of it—of the State, of the human form, or whatever—yet the whole thus represented will only be a reification. The wholeness of an environment, rather, will be whatever it is we function within—even though it cannot be defined or represented. Hence it turns out that communitarian ideologies like Communism and Socialism—and these differ only in the rigour of their idealistic logic—are actually all-embracing only in so far as they are concerned with the distribution of possessions amongst the human race. (And this is a perfectly honourable concern.) But they are not concerned with whether that race should possess the earth: that they do not question. As the disastrous condition of Eastern Europe has shown, these ideologies are part of the problem; they have served only to spread and deepen the roots of materialism—and have done so through a travesty of communality. No more than 'Capitalism', in fact, do these ideologies question Cartesian dualism. (To be fair, western Europe is not essentially different: eastern Europe has fouled its own backyard, western Europe our common seas and atmosphere.)

And ultimately, our efforts to tame environment stem from our conviction that the universe is composed of things, of objects. This is the presumption of atomism, which marks the course in pursuit of reality down which we were so fatefully set by our cultural forebears in Classical Greece. (It is no mere irony that philosophically the 'discoverer' of the atom was called Democritus. He has bequeathed us a politics of atomistic persons—and of alienation.) This view of reality marks the great divide between the civilisations of the West and of the East. For in the East, and at about the same time, this question was also faced and a very different answer reached. In Eastern thought (very briefly) what we in the West take to be objects are seen as but conveniences of speech, part of the conversation of human life, each one existing, not as such, but only as a distinction from others; and what actually is substantial (though it may indeed exist) cannot be spoken of. All our 'objects' are, in fact, reifications. This suggests that the world may, therefore, be better understood in terms of relationships, rather than of separate substances, and is to be regarded as an interdependent whole. The endorsement this view offers of the notion of environment emerging here must increasingly be apparent—*pari passu*, indeed, with the chickens coming home to roost in the West as a result of the atomism which seemed to offer it mastery of the world.

So, after all, to what is it that we are having recourse when we speak of environment? Whatever it is, there would seem to be something strange, even mysterious, about it. It lies beyond where all our mechanistic explanations have to stop; at the boundaries of speech, therefore. (For, as

Wittgenstein very simply admitted, all justifications have to come to an end. Or, in St. Augustine's more complex formulation: 'No one must therefore try to get from me what I know that I do not know, unless, it may be, in order to learn not to know what must be known to be incapable of being known.') Environment thus understood is analogous to the 'forms of life' which are the givens of our thought: that is, the ordinary everyday practices—like sleeping and eating and loving—whose circumstances it would usually be profitless to consider before ever we performed them. It is the ground of our actions. Perhaps, then, it would be better to ask, not what environment substantively is, but rather what kind of appeal to it we are actually making when we call it in aid.

Chapter Four

Language and silence

WHAT KIND OF APPEALS, then, do bankrupts make? It will depend, no doubt, upon whether they know and accept their own bankruptcy. In any case, the metaphor cannot here be taken too far without losing its force. It is enough that it is meaningful to ask such a question. For what surely cannot be disputed is that the last hundred years in the West have seen an expression of despair over our civilisation, unparalleled since the decline of Rome. This desperation first found expression in Neitzche's writings and Spengler's *Decline of the West*—whilst the wars and holocausts of the twentieth century will mark it down in history (if, indeed, there is to be any history) as a period of which humanity will be utterly ashamed. But if this bankruptcy is not yet universally recognised—and it isn't—this must surely be because people still suppose the mechanisms for controlling events—the mechanics of suppressing a tyrant here, or relieving mass starvation there—can continue to be operated, could we but sort out the levers. And they suppose this because they know of nothing but mechanistic thought.

Mechanistic thought concerns the action and reaction, the impact, of one object upon another object. What we are experiencing today is the cumulative consequences of such interactions beyond their intended effects. The implications of this realisation go very deep: as deep as Adam's covenant with God.

It was Adam's trust that when God brought the animals to him to be named, he would thereby possess and rule over them, for by their names he would know what they really were. This covenant was essentially the same as that upon which Descartes relied: that, radically separate though we were from the world about which we thought, God would not deceive us in those thoughts. This separation indeed necessitated God's very existence. And even (or especially) St. Augustine was wrong: we now must admit the child is not, as he supposed, a homunculus, a pre-existent Self, only waiting to acquire language in order to name and control the objects serviceable to itself in the world surrounding it. The upshot, then, is that we can no longer trust language to tell us what is real.

Of course, this recognition is not entirely new. Kant's 'counter-Copernican revolution' of two hundred years ago drew for us the limits of rational thought and showed that Man out of his experience must both invent and sustain his use of those concepts without which he would otherwise be 'precipitated into darkness'. Admittedly, we have wasted those two hundred years with the futile hostilities of solipsism (making ourselves perfect) and idealism (perfecting the world), as of the Romantic movement and social engineering. (Though the majority in our all too complex industrial society have lapsed into a nihilistic amnesia.) But Wittgenstein has now taken us beyond Kant. Kant took us (he believed) to an indefinable Noumenon, the ultimate but inexpressible reality beyond thought. Wittgenstein takes us by means of language (not thought) to assumptions about objects—including any hypothetical Noumenon—as 'neither a something, nor a nothing either'. Language, in other words, simply cannot picture reality for us. To recognise that it cannot do this is to be rid of our most profound illusion.

But in any case the world is such that, increasingly, we are left wondering what is real about it. (It is surely not by coincidence that contemporary philosophy should simply reflect this puzzlement.) It may therefore be helpful to look back a hundred years into the heartland of the old Europe, at the vestiges of the Holy Roman Empire centred on Vienna, from which indeed Wittgenstein himself stemmed. Karl Kraus, the mordant observer of this scene, characterised it as 'the proving-ground of mankind's self-destruction'. It was a scene in which discernment of the real from the apparent was a prime preoccupation—and, we are told, all Viennese at that time were (perhaps necessarily) philosophers. Such an atmosphere must have been conducive to the development of that ultimate nihilist, Hitler—who was in fact a schoolfellow (in Linz) of Wittgenstein, though without their knowing one another. With a dreadful, but apposite, irony it also bred that idealist of Zionism, Hertzl. Tolstoy, with his precepts of repentance and self-sufficiency, was a significant cult figure; and alongside him Vienna revived and adopted the existentialism of Kierkegaard. Truth, in this desperate position, could only be lived; and Wittgenstein himself was to say in the Tractatus, in which he sought to find the limits of what can meaningfully be said, that there are no ethical principles, only ethical actions. Vienna nurtured Freud, of course, and saw, through Loos and before the Bauhaus, the birth of Modern architecture, and through Schoenberg the radicalisation of music. And Einstein was close by. In other words, in a society that was patently out of joint, with new and often alien technology pasted over the fragile fabric of an ancient civilisation, together with the all-pervasive presence of the secret police, that Empire lived ever closer to the brink of all the old certainty.

Today, a hundred years later, Europe at large is playing out the same game. All our certainties are gone. The last of them disappeared in the eastern Europe of 1989. The long retreat of Christianity nears its end. Though materialism seems to hold the field, the black clouds of oil burning over the Persian Gulf are a metaphor for the obscurity in which our pursuit of matter is overshadowing the earth itself. Our abuse of the earth, moreover, is only matched by the terminal decadence of our personal dependence on drugs. And even science, upon which all our certainties have hitherto rested, now informs us that the natural world itself is inherently uncertain.

So can we learn from the experience of the old European cockpit of Vienna? Perhaps there is a germ of a new beginning to be found there. It lies paradoxically in the reception of incomprehensibility given to Wittgenstein's Tractatus (which was in large part compiled during his much-decorated active service in the Great War). The Viennese logical positivists, the ultimate philosophical atomists, made of Wittgenstein their cult figure, but were perplexed by his indifference towards them. He had, indeed, said to one publisher in the course of a long and fruitless search for publication of his book, 'My work consists of two parts: the one presented here plus all that I have not written. And it is precisely this second part that is the important one.' So how do you publish silence—that of which one cannot speak? (In fact, when Wittgenstein did meet with the so-called Vienna Circle, he didn't discuss philosophy but read them the poems of Rabindranath Tagore.) Wittgenstein's friend, Englemann, illuminated the question: 'A whole generation of positivists was able to take Wittgenstein as a positivist, because he has something of enormous importance in common with the positivists: he draws the line beyond what we can speak about and what we must be silent about, just as they do. The difference only is that they have nothing to be silent about. Positivism holds—and this is its essence—that what we can speak about is all that matters in life. Wittgenstein passionately believes that all that really matters in life is precisely what, in his view, we must be silent about.' So what is this silent realm, and how is it peopled?

Perhaps it is where Pan lives? For Pan lives, of course, in panic and pandemonium: in an endemic chaos, that is, where the order humankind has imposed on the world by language does not obtain. The Christians turned Pan into the Devil, though only after the Greeks themselves had ostracised him from the Homeric pantheon by cleaning up the gods' scandalous amorality. For the illiterate common people, however—that is, those who retained their imagination—he long remained the most popular and immanent of the gods. He was there still, along with other vestiges of the language of myth, in Shakespeare's *A Midsummer Night's Dream*, though it was not to be long—about thirty years—before Descartes' rationalism finally banished him. Yet, as our own science starts coming to terms with chaos, perhaps Pan will return. He is to be discerned—and he is not very agreeable—in such writers as Jean Genet and William Golding. His spirit, moreover, is still present in the landscapes apprehended in Chinese geomancy, with its right placing of elements therein, just as it is fundamental to animist traditions like Shinto. (Indeed, it is a nice question as to whether these practices are any more obscure than the pseudo-rational processes of British planning practice.) To speak of Pan as spirit, moreover, is perhaps the most legitimate of devices to enable discourse to be held about what cannot be said: not, that is, of anything but fable. Even nowadays, in fact, it is quite common to speak about the 'spirit of place', and perhaps surprisingly this remains widely acceptable. At all events, whatever the scientific study of chaos may suggest—and to a layman it betrays a certain inherent contradiction—it must be understood that what it is important one should not speak about is not anything 'out there'.

This is not tantamount to nihilism. On the contrary, to 'have nothing to be silent about'—that is nihilism; for that 'nothing' is something which negates what we cannot say. Such nihilism is the pervasive sickness of the West, foreshadowed by Nietzche, in its manifold Fascist guises (not least in its latter-day art). What one cannot speak about, on the contrary, the spiritual abode of Pan, has no reference; it is neither a nothing, nor a something either. The dialogue about it turns back upon language itself: 'It is what human beings say that is true and false; and they agree in the language they use. This is not agreement in opinions but in forms of life.' As Wittgenstein also said: 'Philosophy leaves everything as it is'; and, just as the purpose of philosophy is 'to show the fly the way out of the fly-bottle', it is equally not to show us the way to the Promised Land. Paradoxically or not, this is why in this understanding of silence a hinge might have been formed upon which the doors of our civilisation might yet be turned.

Chapter Five

Of limited wholeness

THIS HINGE OF THOUGHT is now revealing itself in the powerful notion of environment: not environment that is possessed, however, or even measurable, but that is unpossessible. The key to this notion, as also to its compatibility with the realms of silence, lies in our understanding of wholeness: of that, in other words, from which our conventional mode of thought ostensibly reduces things and atomises them.

It is the characteristic of wholeness that it can never be fully understood. We can never understand everything about anything; there will always be assumptions to be made and taken on trust, just as no mathematical proof can be made in its own terms. The meaning of the world lies outside the world, as Wittgenstein said: as also 'Feeling the world as a limited whole—it is this that is mystical.' What lies outside all our experience, but without which that experience could not be had, is sometimes called the ground of our existence—though it is important not to suppose this ground is somehow concrete—and what we think of as environment partakes of the same characteristic, whilst pertaining to more particular circumstances rather than to existence itself.

Perhaps it may help in understanding the point being made here to consider the English countryside. For many people, no environment could be more precious; its preservation is so dear to them they would like to mothball it, and doing this is considered a touchstone of political greenery. Now there is no questioning the spiritual refreshment this environment offers—though it is not the only one in the world with this quality: there are others, of quite different structure, that might also claim it, just as an hypothetical English countryside of smallholders and part-time farmers, say, might have its own quite different charm. But the character we now so appreciate was not intentionally created; rather, it is just a resultant, the accidental consequence of instrumental activities, of agricultural technology and social structure. Indeed, the English countryside is in large measure the residue of a great moral crime—the Enclosures—to say nothing of the devastation of the English forests by our neolithic forebears. Furthermore, in the case of the parklands surrounding many manor houses (perhaps the only countryside that was ever 'planned'), this ideally land-scaped countryside is an ultimate expression of the mentality of the Enlightenment: that is, of the detachment of the observer from the observed, which required the removal of all human presence from a picture of the natural world to be seen from the windows of the great house. In fact, nothing could be more alien than this to the concept of environment being here explored. To create the English countryside, in truth, the peasantry were proletarian-ised—and William Cobbett, that greatest of rural Englishmen, would have much to say about our present-day preservers of it. And, of course, the Highland Clearances tell a still more searing tale.

The English countryside, then, whatever its morality, is an environment that happened and, of course, like all environments, it was bound to happen. All phenomena are interdependent (in the world, if not in the laboratory) and in the world there will be indirect, or secondary, consequences of all intentional actions. Environment can be understood as the compound of such consequences. The courting of two birds, for instance, is their affair; but for us their courting is environmental. But it's only environmental—rather than merely a manifestation of chaos—because it conforms to our notion of some whole: in this case, the countryside. By the same token, well-meaning so-called 'environmental' actions—actions designed to improve the environment—will have their own environmental consequences. The chimneys of coal-fired power stations, for instance, cannot be scrubbed without creating an immense problem of sludge waste-disposal, and that problem will be solved only at further environmental cost, and so on. Likewise, preservation of the countryside as we know it, by some act of policy, must have environmental consequences of its own. That is why the weekend occupation by urban yuppies of the neo-Picturesque villages originally built—as they were in their hundreds—to house the peasantry displaced by the Enclosures, whilst it may preserve the appearance of the countryside, changes its reality completely. Of course, it would be possible to preserve the appearance of this environment by turning farmers into park-keepers, thus simply prolonging the illusions of the eighteenth century gentry, but no one should then suppose that the values of rural life have remained the same.

For similar reasons no one should suppose that environmental questions can be entrusted to scientific solutions, which is a belief to which our political establishment clings. An obvious warning in point is the substitution of nuclear energy for the fossil fuel now polluting the atmosphere. This example, in fact, is the clearest instance of the need at the root of our predicament, not for more knowledge—though this is not to say science, with its partial knowledge, cannot help—but rather for a change of mentality. Or, to put it differently, for a change in science itself. And, of course, it is changing. Einstein may have said, concerning Quantum Theory, 'God does not play dice with the universe'—which echo of Cartesian dualism served as the last act before which the curtain was brought down on the classical epoch of science. But Niels Bohr's reputed refutation of this philosophy, though still but little quoted, is far more cogent: 'There is no quantum world. There is only a quantum-mechanical description. It is wrong to think that the task of physics is to find out how nature is. Physics concerns what we can say about nature.' With this philosophy of science, in fact, the notion of environment being explored here could happily co-exist.

This composition of man and the world, of speaker and what is spoken of, is an attribute of an inherent limitation in our use of language—a limitation that stands in contrast to the assumptions of classical physics, that the potential of language is as limitless as the world it seemingly describes; and a corollary of quantum physics is that environment, which cannot be contrived by any such composition, is strictly useless—as useless as a sunset, or even a painting by Titian. It may help to recall here Wittgenstein's dictum: 'The meaning of a word is its use in the language.' Environment in this perspective, then, would be 'that of which one cannot speak'.

That is to say environment, in fact, is a fundamental challenge to our notion of Self—as much our altruistic as our acquisitive Self: that which stands apart from the world in order to measure and value it. For what this reasoning suggests is that, in relation to the intentional world, environment has no more dimension than, by analogy, the unconscious has relative to the conscious.

Perhaps at this juncture, and as a counterpoise to any implicit downgrading of mechanics in the foregoing, it needs to be said that the wholeness from which our notion of environment stems carries no endorsement of 'holism'.

Holism presumes the completeness of wholes, whereas it is from their incompleteness that environment stems. Failure to recognise this limitation is the Achilles' Heel of 'holism'—and has been so for all Utopias from Plato's Republic down to the present day. Moreover, the concept of 'holism' has done, and could continue to do, great damage to the emerging new paradigm of thought in general. It is the source of the accusations of authoritarianism so often, and with some justice, levelled against Green activists. This is particularly true of self-proclaimed ecologists, for their ecosystems are artificially circumscribed—and justifiably so, no doubt, for some study purposes—by professional edict, rather than as forms of life.

There is a further crucial consequence of the limited character of wholeness, and this concerns the relationship of environment to 'Nature'. It is widely supposed that these are synonymous. 'Nature' commonly represents the ultimate 'thing out there', the effect of all of which God (or the Big Bang, or whatever) was the cause—which for some is as much as to say, the Environment. *The Economist* magazine, for instance, when it brought itself to do a special supplement on the Environment (which is rather like Lucifer taking it upon himself to explain the gospels) preached that preservation of the Environment—i.e., not competing with the industrial West—was very important for Third World countries because they lived off it. In other words, natural resources and environment are supposedly one and the same.

In just the same way, conservation movements in the West are commonly biased in favour of the physical as against the social world, giving instinctive precedence, say, to preservation of the countryside above housing to relieve urban congestion. Yet this 'Nature' is nothing but metaphysical supposition—just such a one, in fact, as Kant warned us against when he said that our reason alone would precipitate us into darkness. 'Nature', as an actual phenomenon, is a prime example of language 'going on holiday': i.e., not working seriously—which is not to say that the metaphoric use of the word is always illegitimate. Hence, if this 'Nature' is a phantom, a shade of Eden, there cannot be any 'balance of Nature' such as our false environmentalists—those who would measure out the Environment, especially to exclude the social world—would like to claim should rule human action. All they are doing in making such claims is, generally speaking, preserving the social status quo. Likewise, the notion of an 'environmental resource' is not just a contradiction in terms—for what then is the environment of this 'resource'?—but some kind of linguistic smokescreen for instrumental action.

So, when all is said and done, when the ropes that have anchored us to our illusions are cut, what is this hinge upon which hopefully our civilisation might yet turn to elude its self-destruction? It would seem to be little more than the hope that there should be no more false promises. But nor can there be any real promises. All the props are gone; the sign-posts have disappeared. All we have is what there is when there is nothing else to refer it to, the very ground of our existence. However, the language-animal, Man, is irrepressible. Even if he cannot speak of that of which he may not speak—the metaphysical—he will speak none the less, even if only of not speaking about it. And, in the end, this is to speak of his environment. To speak of environment, though we cannot specify what it is, is to make an affirmation that our actions are meaningful, that they have a context.

To reach this stage of feeling that what we do has meaning it is necessary to give full weight to the wholeness of things—in current parlance, to our right-brain thinking, or even to our feminine and intuitive side—whilst never supposing that this in itself is all. Thus reached, environment has the quality of the sacred, for it circumscribes knowledge. It is not determinate, nor predictable. It is beyond the bounds of reason, and in it the Self is absorbed. In another parlance, it is spirit as understood by St. John: 'Like the wind that bloweth where it listeth, and you hear the sound thereof, but whence it cometh and whither it goeth, you know not'. For us, in the darkness of these times, that resonates with the trust we are now placing in environment.

Chapter Six

Of spirit, emptiness and environment

OUR RISING CONCERN FOR ENVIRONMENT, then, is a symptom of how meaningless our lives have become. Nor is this surprising when our obsessive pursuit of material growth at best only fouls our own nest and at worst threatens our very survival. We ever more desperately need some context to lend meaning to our way of life; and the danger is, as already said, that we shall only exacerbate our condition by applying the principles of that ever more questionable way of life to the contrivance of such a context—and call it 'the Environment'.

The universalistic pretensions of this concept of the Environment are a product of our governing mentality, which sees the world as 'out there', detached from ourselves as observers of it. This 'out there' syndrome of ours totalises the Environment. But, in fact, there is not one Environment, there are many; there is your and my and our environment, the built, the natural, the moral, the social environment, the urban, the rural environment, and so on: the environments of all our countless forms of life. Nor is there any monolithic environment that is somehow the sum of these. There may indeed be a global environment in so far as it makes sense for us to talk about the globe. but such an environment is *sui generis* and relates only to activities on a global scale. (And Gaia may exist, but it is not the

Environment.) The sum of all our environments is not the Environment.

It is idealism and reductionism, jointly—as with the rational idealism of Descartes—that have conduced to the metaphysical certitudes of our multiple specialisations (each seeking the essence of things) within an enabling and sheltering whole, of which *the* Environment has become the ultimate expression. (Of course, it would be misleading to blame Descartes for all our woes; he only expressed what logically our culture was perhaps bound to make us think.)*The* Environment, then, has become the ultimate expression of this false context of meaning.

By contrast, the environments of all our manifold forms of life are metaphors of the impenetrable reality in which each such form is embedded. In this sense environment is the medium between spirit and matter: or, put conversely, spirit is that without which matter has no meaning, and to speak of environment is to say where spirit is, to give it a home. Any description of an environment can only be arbitrary and in self-referring terms. An urban environment, for example, can only be spoken of in terms of such criteria—of housing density, or traffic volume, or crime rates—as we have agreed in order to discuss whatsoever is 'urban'; but any such discussion can only be in reference to that agreement. Or, just possibly, it might be in poetic terms—as, say, one might describe the countryside—for such terms are also self-referential: a poem is its own meaning and is a unique form of expression.

If this perspective of environment—as the home of spirit—should at first be hard to grasp, it is perhaps because, ever since Democritus posited the atom and our Hellenistic forebears so fatally started us on the search for the substance, the matter, of the world, with an ever-accelerating speed we have contrived a world so fragmented as to be meaningless. Meaning depends upon context: by abstracting a part from whatsoever it belongs to, though our knowledge of that part may thereby increase, yet what that knowledge means will not grow. Indeed, if we pursue that knowledge for its own sake, its meaning may even diminish as a result of losing sight of the subject's context in life, and its inexorable replacement merely by the power which knowledge confers. It could be held, in fact, that this substitution—of the power of knowledge for the wealth of life—accounts for the sterility of our culture.

Nevertheless, one can already hear the protests over this perspective of environment as the home of spirit. Is it for this that we must renounce certainty? Are there to be no bearings on these shifting sands of language—of poetry, even? This implies mystery and, though the world may be complex, yet is it therefore inherently mysterious? Surely, in this age of the computer, it is not inconceivable that some hyper-computer could tell us what the effects and the side-effects and the side-effects of the side-effects of all the relationships constituting an environment might be, till nothing is left to be explained. Yet, in simple truth, even at the humdrum level, causation itself is mysterious.

The classical discussion of causation need not be rehearsed here: of how can a necessary connection be perceived between one state of affairs and another: how one state of affairs can become a different state of affairs without its already being that other state of affairs. Suffice it to cite the conclusion of the classic philosopher of causation, David Hume: 'We are entirely determined by custom when we conceive an effect to follow from its usual cause.' Or again: 'In reality, there is no part of matter that does ever, by its sensible qualities, discover any power or energy, or give us ground to imagine that it could produce any thing, or be followed by any other object, which we could denominate its effect. Solidity, extension, motion;

these qualities are all complete in themselves, and never point out any other event which may result from them. The scenes of the universe are continuously shifting, and one object follows from another in an uninterrupted succession; but the power of force which actuates the whole machine is entirely concealed from us, and never discovers itself in any of the sensible qualities of body.' Events, he says, are 'conjoined', but never 'connected', except by our habits of thought. Hume's time-bomb ticked away for some two hundred years whilst the West wasted its resources on the futile conflicts of determinism—whether of Marxism, or capitalism, or romaticised fascism—but he has received his vindication with the emergence out of the bosom of science itself of the principle of Uncertainty. Pan, it would seem, lives amongst us after all, and his spirit is as real as matter: indeed, these are part and parcel of each other.

This is not to say, of course, that spirit any more than environment is something 'out there', or even that we can call upon 'the spiritual' for our salvation. Should we be tempted to think this it is because we are inured to the separation of spirit and matter; our dualism conditions us to it. God and Caesar rule separate realms, and the story of Christ driving the money-changers from the temple epitomises this. We applaud that triumph of pure spirit over basest matter. None the less, in truth, the money-changers in the temples of the classic world were there as of right. Indeed, the temples were built around them, rather than the case being that they occupied and soiled hallowed ground. For, prior to literacy, one gave one's oath upon any uncertain transaction, and did so on sacred ground. Literacy, when it came, only served to generate an illusory certainty, and so to dispense with the sacred; for, actually, the written word no more describes reality (and perhaps, by the illusions it raises, less so) than does the spoken.

For example, when Westerners arrived in Japan demanding written contracts, there were virtually no lawyers to be found. Indeed, there are still very few in that country, relatively speaking. The atomisation of the world in legal language is not congenial to the Japanese way of business, which sees as important the context of any transaction as much as the transaction itself. If the Japanese have anything to teach the West, perhaps this is it. Maybe the ancient rituals of the City of London are the nearest we come to it.

Our resistance, then, in acknowledging the uncertainty that seems inseparable from spirit is cushioned by our equation of the spiritual with the religious, yet only serves to exacerbate the confusion between these. Religion supplies us with all its certainties and is, to this extent, the natural ally of materialism—as Church is of State. This is why the notion of environment is antipathetic to both, for it knocks away the props of Cartesianism upon which they both stand: as much detachment from a fragmented world, as our belief that that detachment will not impair our knowledge of it. Of course, by copying science's methods of proof in its assertion of certainty, religion has discredited itself, perhaps permanently. The existence of God can never be proven as the provisional truths of science can be established. But by any standard the certitudes of doctrine, ritual, dogma and hierarchy have as little to do with the spirit as any supposed certainties of the environment have to do with our silence about that whereof one cannot speak.

The confusion between religion and the spiritual has indeed become pervasive in our culture. It extends to the Common Law, for instance, where for this reason it is sometimes quite unclear what is or is not charitable at law. This kind of decision would seem, even more than usual, to depend upon the judge before whom one might find oneself and, probably, on his early moral upbringing. Should you wish to make a charitable bequest to the closed

Carmelite Order, you would find the House of Lords has already decided that a life of prayer is not in the public interest. The ethos of materialism could surely go no further than this; it is as much as to say the notion of environment is worthless if it cannot be materialised and measured, or that whatever is inherently inexplicable may not be recognised. Descartes' proposition, of course, was that God would not deceive us—and, to make sure he doesn't, we try to deal, not in intangibles, but in the grossest reality. But, in so doing, we only risk deceiving God.

Yet there is one religious tradition that is congenial to the notion of environment being developed here. This is Buddhism. Sadly, in fact, it has to be said that the whole tenor of this discussion fits more readily into a framework, not of Western, but rather of Eastern ideas—though one would gladly make an exception for the tradition of Christian mystics such as Meister Eckhart and the author of *The Cloud of Unknowing*. One can, alas, hardly say as much for the honest scepticism of a David Hume, for that comes too close to fuelling the West's despair. The distinction between West and East is more radical even than his thought could span; for what the West treats of unquestioningly as things, the East understands as reifications.

Emerging out of the Western tradition, however, albeit out of the ruins of its system of logic, there is developing a strain of thought very compatible with Buddhism. It is the mark of Wittgenstein's genius—as of his immediate significance for us—that single-handed he effectively re-drew the map of non-dualistic thought, much as Nagarjuna, the greatest of Buddhist philosophers and of whom Wittgenstein actually knew nothing, had drawn it nearly two thousand years before. (This parallel has now been described by a widening circle of scholars, pre-eminently by Chris Gudmunsen in his *Wittgenstein and Buddhism*.) The Middle Way of the classic philosophy, for instance—that is, between realism and nihilism, objectivity and subjectivity—is echoed in Wittgenstein's 'neither a something, nor a nothing either'. Rather than any notion of the Creation, at the core of Nagarjuna's thought is the idea (poorly translated, but we are at the mercy of the reasonances of our vocabulary) of 'emptiness'. This expresses our awareness that, though we are in the midst of causation, ultimately we cannot say what it is: the dialectic of language will always exhaust itself and there will be no thing for another thing to be referred to. 'Emptiness' has an affinity with Wittgenstein's ultimate 'forms of life': what we are left with when, as is bound to be the case, any explanation, any language game, comes to an end—that of which one must be silent. And it seems to me this is what nowadays, in the impasse to which our pursuit of knowledge has led us, people aspire to when they invoke the notion of environment.

If this is so, if despite our mental conditioning to define a thing where no things are, then environment has simply become an expression of our search for meaning in a meaningless world. As such, this expression is truly a spiritual phenomenon. By the same token, as must by now be evident, it is tantamount to a renunciation, implicitly or explicitly, of the major premises of our Western mode of thought: of atomism, of the Creation, of the soul, of the mind, of Heaven and Earth, of God and Caesar, of knowledge as power and of wealth as a store of goods. Is this to expect too much? It depends, not just on how serious you think our problems are, but whether they are self-induced, and induced by misconceptions of a great profundity: whether it matters, therefore, that habitation of great areas of this huge globe are at risk, and that the winds of greed have already started to rage around us. If all this does matter, then a true understanding of environment is not a theoretical question but a practical one, and urgent.

Chapter Seven

Environmental politics?

So WHAT IS TO BE DONE? What is to follow so wholesale a rejection of our stock-in-trade of ideas? Granted that our culture has devalued environment and, short-sightedly, has pursued and promoted only whatsoever is specific—has, in effect, only believed in the specific, even being blind to the value to the specific of what lies around it—what guidelines should we now follow concerning environment? What, in other words, should be the politics of environment? And what would be their sociology?

To anyone who has followed the discussion so far a difficulty must candidly be faced over this question. Politics, it might be agreed in the first place, is about power and how power is used. Indeed, as between these—power for its own sake, that is, and power used to achieve some goal—no categoric distinction need (not, at least, at this juncture) be made. Power, of itself, is a necessary means for the Self to manipulate the world; it is a main expression of dualism, of the separation of the Self from the world. The legendary egoism of politicians is almost by itself sufficient testimony to this. Politics, then, determines who shall possess what. All this being said, however, no environment can be possessed. How, then, is there to be a politics of environment?

Perhaps this difficulty explains why some people can sympathetically say that, whilst there is a place for the spiritual in Green philosophy, this cannot be extended to politics. If this is so, however, it would seem to leave any

Green party in a vacuum—and in a much greater vacuum than, say, a Christian Democratic party, which has the tenets of its belief to draw upon. Yet, certainly, an environment cannot be possessed; and any attempt to possess it—as NIMBY environmentalism so blatantly does—will merely turn an environment into a chattel. By the same token, moreover, the pejorative charge associated with 'pollution' makes of this something heavily value-laden and redolent of abused power. Perhaps, then, the assumption of an environmental politics has to be that there is an ideal environment, one which it must be the business of politics to realise; and that, likewise, there is a kind of pollution from the elimination of which there would be no losers—and maybe this hypothesis might be used to distinguish pollution from mere nuisance?

One wonders, however, how this could be so? Conceivably, in some situation, all the human beings concerned might benefit from the elimination of some contamination affecting all of them, and the offensive substance (or whatever) might be absorbed into the natural world. Then, presumably, Nature itself would be the loser? But Nature, surely, does not pollute Nature; it is no less natural in one manifestation than in another. To be rid of pollution, then, we humans might with impunity, and in defence of our own interests, violate the natural world in whatever way we needed to sustain our way of life. In other words, in this scenario, we would be left with the old humanistic values. These are the values that follow from the dualism of humankind separate from the world around us. They are also such as sanction the resolution in human terms of the differences—the in-built differences—between ourselves; for what divides us as much as it unites us is our humanity: that is, the ways in which we organise ourselves.

But, if these humanistic values are all that we are left with, and if 'pollution' is to be part of them, some bits of Nature

THE FABRIC OF THE WORLD

must somehow be more natural than others. Excessive carbon dioxide in the atmosphere, for instance, is actually repugnant to us only because it threatens humankind. There is thus no more humanistic a notion than 'pollution'. Moreover, and because it is a function of humanism, some of us will think we have more to lose from pollution than others—which will make any action over it politically charged; the incidence of global warming will certainly not be uniform. 'Pollution', according to this reasoning, then, simply means fouling our own nest. So we perhaps shouldn't deceive ourselves that it ultimately refers to some ideal state of Nature.

In truth, however, that is just what it must do if it is to make any political sense. And nothing could be more conducive to this metaphysical exercise than the workings of power. Politics, indeed, is the very playground of idealism. At least as we experience it—as conducted in large units, in the nation state—politics generates an illusion of wholeness. The very size of these political units virtually forces idealism upon their participants; such a framework for the dualism of power calls for idealisations simply in order to make sense of the exercise of that duality. That is to say, only the essence of the matter could seemingly be comprehended on that scale of activity.

And, of course, people must combine in any such pursuit of power; each Self must be incorporated into a political party, and the parties must subscribe to the rules governing the pursuit of power. It will then help, but it is not essential, if the common ground of each such party is ideologically given; but there are limits to what people, even quite cynically, can hold in common, and so in practice the requisites of power itself are the main binding force of any political party. Thus, no Green party could gain and keep power without participating in such political manoeuvres, and all such participation would require compromises in that party's common ground.... unless, that is, it enforced an ideology: that is to say, presumably, some idealisation of the state of Nature.

Put like this, then, the prospect for a politics of environment indeed seems hopeless: or worse than hopeless, positively evil. To compress all the variety of the natural world into some metaphysical essence, and then demand obedience to it, is close to sacrilege. And of course there is nothing amiss with compromise, per se, or with allying oneself with others over one issue or another. One's integrity is not normally deemed compromised in so doing. But it is, to say the least, disingenuous to do so in the name of environment if that carries an implication of absolute value. If somebody's smoky factory, or even Kuwait's burning oil fields—that portent of our fate—pollutes my surroundings, I am actually only saying that I prefer the world ordered without that disruption to it. The temptation this offers me, however, is to project that preference onto an idealisation of life called 'the Environment'. In this way Green idealism risks becoming the ultimate travesty of ideological politics.

This being so, is one not forced to conclude that environmental politics cannot be—or, at least, should not be—pursued? Before one admits to such a counsel of despair, however, one would do well to consider the spirit in which politics is conducted. It may be that in that spirit we shall find the approach we are seeking. Environment, after all, is where spirit resides.

All politics is conducted in some spirit or another, no matter how rational it might suppose itself to be. Indeed, the greater its fabricated certitudes—the more absolute its ideology—the more vulnerable it will be to spiritual collapse. 'Conviction' politics, the politics that denies its opponents any legitimacy—and which is so lamentably demonstrated in the confrontational politics of the House of Commons—is merely spiritually impoverished; it lives off the excrement of its own insults. But, however poor in spirit, it will not, it cannot, lack spirit as such.

A further corollary of a politics that supposes itself free of any spiritual context is an easy tolerance of centralised power. The more patently materialistic is politics—the more blatantly it is a matter of competing economic interest groups—the easier must it be to achieve a concentration of power: as, for instance, in the nation state. This tendency is simply a consequence of 'extension'—to use the Cartesian term for the characteristic that distinguishes the world from the Self. That is to say, we are talking here about the quantitative rather than the qualitative: hence about the ease of manipulation of the measurable—a feature of materialism that stems from the uniformity of all phenomena susceptible to measurement. A society governed by materialism and its concomitant technology is simply spiritually dessicated; but it will have a spirit of sorts, none the less, though its myths may by any standard seem strange: the myth of 'growth', for instance, with its augury of men's hopeless restlessness.

The spread and hold of bureaucracy are indeed the hallmarks of a society whose politics are shamelessly materialistic. The bureaucratic is simply another category in the catalogue of attributes of any politics which likes to think it is in no way spiritual. And of course bureaucracy is indispensable for the regulation of all the traffic—literal and figurative—which technology generates: the traffic of television channels, or genetic engineering, or whatever. Bureaucracy in this respect is a veritable surrogate of the spirit: the medium in which all things travel. In such circumstances the power of the State spreads inexorably, whatever the party in power and even if that party announces it will reduce the power of the State. All political parties in a high technology culture are party to the centralisation of power. This applies equally to the 'hidden hand' of the market, which may not itself be bureaucratic but which will all the more effectively spread the territory of 'extension' that will require bureaucratic regulation. (No one has yet suggested—not even the most devoted 'disciple of Adam Smith'—that the decision whether to pass on the left or the right hand side of the road should be left in every instance to the driver making the highest bid. Yet the more cars the market generates the greater become the problems of regulating the traffic.) So the spirit of such a politics is merely entombed in its society; and the spirit of reason, as Kant taught us long enough ago, is characteristically blind to its own limitations.

The problem for an environmental politics, then, if such a politics could exist at all, is to discover a radically different spirit in which it might be practised. Such a spirit would not be of religion, with its dogma and given beliefs, nor (above all) of idealism, with all the attributes of power that go integrally therewith. Yet, if such a politics is to be environmental, it must be concerned with wholes and not with the parts by which reductionism, in the guise of the Ministry of this sector and of that, breaks down the nation state into manageable bits. Yet the wholes with which an environmental politics should be concerned must, like all forms of life, be limited. They can have no pretensions to being absolute, nor all-inclusive of life. Their wholeness may perhaps seem mystical, but actually it is only pragmatic.

What all this points to, surely (and the analogy with a similar concept in contemporary physics may or may not be coincidental), is local life. That is to say, it directs attention to the paramount importance of the politics of cities, towns and villages. In Britain this is not the same thing as local government. Local government in Britain is simply a misnomer for a delegation of powers from the centre: a matter of administrative convenience. (This explains why local elections in Britain attract a farcical 30% turn-out of electors. In France, which is supposedly so centralised but which in fact still draws on the long tradition of power in the commune, the equivalent figure is 80%. Britain, one may reflect, is still under Norman occupation.) The spirit in which an environmental politics might be practised, rather, is one which—paradoxically or not, given the pervasive nature of environment—would accompany a dismantling of the centralised state as we know it.

In all logic, indeed, there can be no place for any Green party in the nation state as it exists; the two are simply incompatible, and any such party will be mocked and torn apart—as some in Europe already have been—by the pursuit of power in any such system. Power in the nation state, after all, is in the service of knowledge and its spirit, not of meaning. The only function, if any, of a Green party in the present political system can be a constitutional one: to enforce an abdication of the centre. As a rule of thumb, whenever a political entity such as a state becomes so big that parties begin to form permanently within it, it is time to stop it growing.

Of course, politics in any such local framework cannot be deterministic. No one could pretend to know what the full implications of any policies in this framework might be, or whether they met any abstract ethical criteria. At least, however, they would knowingly be probabilistic—unlike, say, the education policies, or the agricultural policies, or the energy policies, or the economic policies, or any other of the functionally determined policies of the nation state with their spurious certitudes stemming from their reductionistic premises. For what, all in all, is the nation state but a machine for exploiting the power of reductionist knowledge?

Now there will no doubt be those who say that this prescription for a truly local politics—one which would not judge of matters functionally (as to whether, say, a village sewage system was technically the last word, or whether a secondary school's catchment area was big enough to support all the subjects under the educational sun), but rather as to how they fitted the pattern of some community—such people will say this prescription is not practicable. Technology, they will say, would not allow of it. Indeed, the effects of technology spread inexorably, on an ever-widening scale. The boundaries of states were not conceived to encompass the environmental effects of present-day technology, any more than they were devised with Scud missiles armed with nuclear warheads in mind.

Precisely! Then would it not be sensible to dismantle these dinosauric bodies devised for confrontations that have long since ceased to signify anything? What relevance do the boundaries of any nation state have to global warming, say, or to depletion of the ozone layer? They are positively injurious to the situation, for they were conceived with confrontation, not co-operation, in mind. All the structures built into and facilitated by nation states are committed to the dualistic exploitation of the world. They are the greatest hindrance to a real politics of environment. Such a politics is one of cooperation, and this is precisely one that the limited wholes of local political life would be (though with no guaranteed certainty of success) best designed to follow, for without cooperation with one another—not to maximise their Gross Domestic Products, but to keep their environments benign—they could not survive.

Technology, of course (unlike the nation state), cannot be disinvented. Indeed, it will doubtless continue to develop so long as our curiosity gets the better of us. However, the technology compatible with politics on a human scale, such as we are speaking of, would be what Schumacher called 'appropriate technology'. Appropriate technology is usually thought of in a Third World context as a way to rescue 'underdeveloped' countries from slavery to high-tech methods and all that they imply. In truth, however, its most serious application should be in a First World that has come to its political senses. Alternative technology—whether for generating power, for benign crop control, or for waste disposal, etc., etc.—is, in fact, very sophisticated; and what it is appropriate to is the emergence of a culture rediscovering the paramouncy of community over monetary values, and which has learnt that a civilisation dedicated to the subject-object idea of knowledge, that is concerned with the parts rather than the whole, with substance rather than relationship, with the specific rather than the environmental—that such a society will be condemned, in a sick parody of democracy, to the concentration of ever more centralised control, and will be petrified by our realisation that this centre has lost control of all our destinies.

Others will say, no doubt, that this prescription of politics on a human scale, even if practicable, would not be desirable. It could only limit everybody's choice; in the pejorative sense of the word, it would be parochial. The plethora of choice, the argument goes, is what enriches the thin sauce of our lives. But who is it who chooses? Was Balaam's ass the richer for his choice? And is someone with fifty television channels to chose from even the same person as he who has but one? The conventional view of choice posits it as an implicit good and presupposes the isolated individual as the chooser—and our prejudice in favour of individuality completes the exercise. Yet, as social beings in a society that offers fifty television channels, what evidence is there that, in terms of Ruskin's dictum that 'the only wealth is life', we are any richer than if we had only one to choose from? The only real question of choice, surely, is about cultural quality, not about more of this or more of that; and this again is best addressed where qualitative rather than quantitative questions are at home—in politics on a human scale. As things are, it too often seems that choice impoverishes rather than enriches us.

More important even than all the foregoing considerations, and a consequence of the uncertainty that must attend any politics conducted in a spirit compatible with environmental concern, is a realisation that such a politics would have a strong moral thrust: that is to say, a concern for values. Logically, after all, if it is accepted that we cannot know what the environmental consequences of our intentional actions are—if, indeed, as argued here, such uncertainty is just where environment is to be found—on what could the justification for those actions come to rest but on moral grounds?

Now it may well be true, as Wittgenstein said (and as Neitzche more vehemently asserted), that there are no moral principles, only moral actions—and, incidentally, Wittgenstein himself appropriately lived the most morally tortured of lives—and therefore we are only exchanging one set of unknowns (the environmental) for another (the ethical). But this is not to deny ethical, any more than environmental, reality: only to say that each case must be decided on its merits. It it certainly not to say that we must return to anything so facile as the disaster of 'Victorian values'—which were, in fact, little to do with Victorianism, being but the product of the Purity Campaign in only the last years of the nineteenth century—in exchange for the equal disaster of the amorality of the present day. What it is to say, rather, is that an environmental politics must actually not be a politics of 'the Environment' but of doing what seems right. And the only context in which this makes environmental sense is the local one, for that is the only place where the Self cannot stand apart from the world and theorise about it as if it were a mere abstraction.

Put simply, one does not wittingly foul one's own nest. But, assuming we must reject the simplistic notion that whatever is in my interests is in the general interest—the 'what's good for General Motors is good for the USA' syndrome—how are the interests of the local whole to be determined? I think the clue to this question lies in the notion of aesthetics. In today's politics, of course, and in most environmental debates, aesthetics is marginalised. (A major exception to this would be the sense of beauty and of awe evoked in those who have seen the earth from space.) In the new paradigm of politics, however, aesthetics would be central. That marks the difference between a possible future and the impossible present.

Aesthetic decisions—and by this I mean participatory actions, not the judgements of observing critics—are made by those involved in the action. Since the actor cannot be dissociated from the action, such decisions must concern the whole of whatever is being decided. (It is only by being detached that the observer can fragment a whole into its parts.) An aesthetic decision is concerned with rightness, appropriateness, etc. It is, however, not merely subjective—nor, therefore, is it something made by some Self or other—but rather stems from our common culture and our language. Certainly, it is as much to do with the feelings as the intellect (should anyone still insist upon distinguishing these) and is at least partly an intuitive or, in the current jargon, a right-brain activity. Nor, above all, is a sense of the aesthetic confined to that by now largely marginalised activity of 'the arts'. There assuredly exists a sense of what is socially harmonious, just as in the Buddhist lexicon there is a concern for 'right livelihood'. Conversely, the slag heaps of the Industrial Revolution and Cobbett's Great Wen (London) were in their time clear offences against the proprieties of life, and hence against their environment, just as high-rise housing of the urban poor has been in our own time. Only the application of universalistic theories to society at large could have allowed such offences to the environments of local life to be made.

Environmentalism today, in fact, is not far short of becoming Humanism on another plane; it would even embrace the sheer contradiction of Green materialism. And, equally, this is why one must be distrustful of all attempts—now so modish, as the Establishment seeks to embrace the cause of 'the Environment'—to quantify and generalise 'environmental impact'. How hard it will be for these latter-day Humanists—the Not in Humanity's Back Yard tendency, who do not recognise humanity's dependence on all the rest—to accept that no common measure for human decisions exists! Nothing could so much invalidate the grand social visions to which they would force us to submit. But how beneficial it will prove that plenty of scope for disagreement must exist over the aesthetics of local politics!

Implicit in these remarks, then, is the notion that for aesthetics (in its wider sense) to be the dominant consideration of environmental politics, our political units must be sufficiently small for the participants to be directly involved. Small is beautiful indeed! It is precisely a legacy of the old paradigm, however, that it has left us with giantist structures of every kind. It is by no coincidence that this is especially true of the historical leader of liberal democracy, Great Britain. Britain is now particularly handicapped in making the transition to a politics centred on local life. At the Norman Conquest Britain was deprived of its communes and began the long process of centralised control, eventually through the House of Comm(u)ons. In compensation, admittedly, the country was left with the marvellously irrational instrument of the Common Law, which over the centuries and through the Justices of the Peace gave some substance to its local life—and which arguably was a far greater bequest to the USA than the

Enlightenment's political forms. So far as local government in Britain is concerned, however, this is but a Victorian invention of administrative convenience, and one is tempted to suggest that, in some kind of national jeu d'esprit, all its cards could with impunity be thrown up in the air just to see where by chance they might land and who would be governing what. But, of course, this state of affairs—and, in particular, the giantism of London and other amorphous conurbations—is only symtomatic of the mentality of the old paradigm, with its thoughts, institutions, language, by which we are held captive. The expectation must be that of themselves these old structures will dissolve—as, for instance, both the radical reversal of two hundred years of rural depopulation and the changing form of 'London' have already started to show.

The logic of the new paradigm, conversely, is that its politics would not be ideologically determined and therefore would not take place in structures where ideology could take root. The mechanistic power plays of fixed political parties would have no place in such a politics. The norm would be something much closer to the 'issues politics' with which nowadays we are becoming increasingly familiar, and which imply a kaleidoscopic flux of ever-changing power groupings. The Whips Office in the House of Commons—that ultimate degradation of a supposedly individualistic political culture—would become a fossilised curiosity. An environmental politics would likewise say goodbye to the false whole of any Utopia; its wholes would be real, but patently limited. On the wider plane, and conventionally speaking, this is to talk in confederate, rather than federal, terms. It is frankly to hold up Switzerland—the only non-nation state in Europe—as the constitutional role model: but also to say that we cannot rely on Switzerland's valleys and mountains to produce the same effect on our own local life.

Let no one claim, however, that whilst Switzerland may be all very well for the Swiss, yet women don't even have the vote there, etc. The influence of women nationally may be small, but likewise who even knows the name of the Swiss Prime Minister? In fact, the central government of that country only exercises such powers and spends such funds as the cantons and communes say it shall have—and these bodies themselves are far smaller than their British equivalents. Yet in the cantons and communes, where power actually lies, representation is just about evenly balanced between the sexes. Feminist politics should surely take much greater note of the question of scale: largeness of scale equals male dominance.

It is likewise to say that the trouble with the European Community is not so much that it threatens to create a new super-state as that, in its coming about, the powers of existing nation states will not be passed down to more local levels: that we will thus be saddled with a doubled centralisation of power. Should this confederate prescript fly in the face of conventional wisdom—of the history of the United States of America, for example—so be it! The constitutional forms of the present-day world are, like so much else, logical consequences of the mentality of the Enlightenment. The Declaration of Independence, so rightly revered, is the supreme expression of this. But it is that logic which now threatens our survival.

To talk in this vein may seem just fanciful—or at best unrealistic—and one must admit to a certain truth in this. For, so long as things go on as they are—which means, so long as GNP goes on rising at a politically satisfactory rate per annum—no amount of talk will persuade any significant numbers of people that nation states must be dismantled: not even if it is explained that GNP takes no account of the capital of the earth. After all, if the grotesque events in the Persian Gulf do not arouse any fundamental questioning of the values we abide by that could justify so singular an action—and they would seem not to have done so—what effect could any kind of talking have?

Well, as Wilfred Owen said before he died in the Great War (that curtain-opener to all the catastrophes of our century): all the poet can do is warn. In environmental politics we are indeed in the business of poetry, but poetry has been sidelined in our culture—and with good reason. Poetry is too powerful and disruptive. In classical Greece 'poet' meant 'maker'; but Plato percipiently banned poets from his Republic, and poetry has been banished from our politics ever since. It is all too liable to see into the heart of the matter, through all theoretical reasoning and idealisation. No member of the Establishment wants to be told 'things fall apart/the centre cannot hold'. Let us at least hope, then, that the Green Party, if it survives at all, will remain as it is, the only source of poetry in our politics; that it will never lose the faculty of innocence and ability to truly speak. For the time being, though, we must acknowledge that here we are engaged in a different language game.

Hence, if the relevance of the foregoing is to be seen at all, it will be through events rather than by intellectual persuasion . It is all too likely that these events will occur. The fabric of our world as we have made it is not meant to withstand the shocks to which it is ever more exposed. Our world is the product of a belief in certainty and, as a result, is far too delicately balanced, too brittle, to withstand the uncertainties—the economic earthquake, say, or the environmental catastrophe—inherent in our fragmentation of it. Nor—and it is all part of the same condition—were the frontiers of nation states designed with Scuds carrying nuclear warheads in mind. In fact, it is fear of such events that may prove the best hope of generating a general change of mentality before, rather than after, some disaster strikes: fear, rather than moral persuasion.

Fear may not be the best of teachers; we cannot, in retrospect, be unreservedly grateful to the fear which turned the Roman world over to Christianity in what was perhaps the only historically comparable circumstances. Almost certainly it gravely distorted the teaching of Christ, and let Original Sin in by the back door. But our circumstances today do not admit of the luxury of much discrimination. It is urgent that we dismantle that pollution-generating machine, the nation state. The best we can do, however, if we are not again to take the life-denying road that was prescribed nearly two thousand years ago, is to issue as much warning as possible of the changes in our lifestyles that our too-long indifference to environment, our fixation on positivism, will surely impose on us.

In brief, we have to achieve government on a human scale. Such a scale is one in which democracy is, in fact, a reality—not the hypocritical farce of elective dictatorship which it now inevitably passes for. It might be thought, however, that the human scale of government is incompatible with the ever wider impact of environmental concerns that know no boundaries, even of states on the present inhuman scale. But this thought serves only to show how insidious has been the idea of 'the Environment' and its equivalence with Nature. The very problem of environment seems to have arisen with the growing scale of our activities. Yet, of course, there is not one environment, but many, even innumerable ones. And environments are not things 'out there' that lie within the writ of governments. They can of course be affected, with various degrees of uncertainty, by the actions of governments—whether fiscal or regulatory—just as in an interdependent universe everything affects everything else. But a larger scale of government is not the key to effective environmental action; indeed, the larger the scale the greater might be the miscalculations, the failure to get to the heart of the matter. Cooperation between smaller-scale governments is arguably the better recipe for this exercise in uncertainty, since their responsibilities must be more concrete, more located in identifiable place and less dependent on ideology. Scale is indeed of paramount importance for environment, but in the opposite sense to what is all too commonly supposed.

All this is only as much as to say that we shall not get from the old paradigm to the new mechanistically. A mere change in the structures of government will not save us from ourselves, for how is that change itself to come about? In truth, everything has to change. For some people, recognising this, it signifies that we must all undergo some inner transformation. This, however, is but the last despairing counsel of the old solipsism that has long contested the roost with idealism. We may, or may not, all change inwardly, depending upon whether you suppose there's any important distinction to be made between our inwardness and our outwardness. There is, however, an all-pervasive change to be made affecting each and all of us: that is, in the language we use—not just in its words, but in their use, their meanings. Two thousand years and more of the premises of dualistic thought—starting, say, with the dualism of good and evil, and culminating in the intense scientific indoctrination of the last four centuries—has left us bewitched by its vocabulary. If one thing is now becoming clear it is that this vocabulary is ripe for deconstruction. There can be no change, political or otherwise, except *pari passu* with a consequent change in our grammar.

Chapter eight

Words and the world

OF COURSE, words change their meanings by usage, not by prescription. The task of philosophy may be, as Wittgenstein says, to save our intelligence from bewitchment by language, but if, as he also says, the meaning of a word is its use in the language, there is probably not much more philosophy can do than cast its bread upon the waters. Where the winds and tides carry its work—what happens when the intellectual thrall of some word is broken—is unpredictable. Nevertheless, in the crisis of these times, we must surely do what we can to break the spell of language by which we have bewitched ourselves and sown the seeds of our own destruction.

In that spirit, then, it is the interpretation words have received under the influence of Cartesianism—of reductionist thought and of the detachment of observer, of the Self, from observed—to which we should direct attention. Such words are no doubt myriad, but it may serve to consider a few that are dominant in our lives. These are concepts which through usage have lost their context and now treat of matters as though they are specialisms independent of their environment. They are all ripe for deconstruction.

Let us first consider words and our feelings, with reference especially to the notion of sexuality. A suitable text to introduce this could be the statement by an African chief to a District Commissioner of the Empire, in the late 19th century: 'It is all this thing called love. We do not understand it at all. This thing called love has been introduced.' It was no doubt the institutional order the British sought to impose on Africa to which this thing called love seemed a key, and above all the institution of monogamous—and heterosexual at that—marriage, which so baffled the chief. In this, he would have had the sympathy of a large part of humankind, both historically (as also prehistorically) and everywhere in the world. The arrangements under which members of the human race have organised the expression of their feelings for one another—not even excluding same-sex marriage—are almost innumerable in their variety. There is no one key to it—and certainly not love. And even in the minority world of Christianity, love has known manifold interpretations, as have also the feelings that have been proscribed in that world. 'Spiritual friendship', alas, is nowadays little more than a euphemism for feelings that have become taboo in the world.

In this connection it would perhaps not be too much to say that the ultimate tragedy of our atomistic worldview is not the obscenity of nuclear power, say, or even the gross materialism that goes hand in hand with our fragmented individualism: it is, rather, the emotional deprivation we have brought upon ourselves. We survive in a landscape of dead words, like a mental Hiroshima. In this atomised world, in the end, we are but the roles we play; we have no other fulfillment. We are abstracted thereby from other experience; we follow the rules our roles prescribe. The alienated, emotionless bureaucrat is the model.

If it be asked how this could consort with the historical Christian notion of the person as a whole being, it has to be said that that notion posited someone withdrawn from the world. The Christian person, though whole, originally denied the world. By the Middle Ages, however, sufficiently long after the trauma of the fall of Rome, the world had become orderly enough to encourage a Christian's cautious involvement in it; and it was to the idea of Nature, to the archetype of Eden, that he first had recourse to restrain arbitrary temporal power in that world. And, so far as sexual relations were concerned, this rule of Nature amounted to the practice of intercourse only for the purposes of procreation (much as today this might surprise anyone familiar with cows bulling). Within this safe definition of Nature, the Self, progenitor of the person, could find a continuing security against the manifold intrusions of the world to which it remained so vulnerable. Thus it is not hard to trace a subsequent transition from monasticism to science: a synonymous exclusion of life, of withdrawal from it, in the monk's cell and the scientist's laboratory respectively. The cultivation of the Self provides their common thread. But the logic of such a process of exclusion of the world is to delineate a person by how he or she plays an allotted part in a world ordered by the laws of some higher Authority. The Self, in terms of this metaphysical reality, is thus (like the atom) irreducible, yet unique and structurally invariant. It is a thing in itself, a compound of attributes conforming to a norm. In the case of children, for instance, this is true whether of Locke's homunculus, who is like a clean slate waiting to be written on, or Rousseau's notion of the child as a child.

In consequence our culture, as it has grown more diffuse, has treated the emotions ever more clinically. They are seen as the properties of anyone's health or sickness, and essentially private. Deviations from the norm of behaviour, from the rules, must be isolated for clinical analysis; and such an analysis will logically posit an innate sexual disposition in any given person. These days, for sure, promiscuity and extra-marital sexual relations are activities which people have largely taken into their own hands, and are symptoms of the breakdown of authority in our culture; but the conditioning of our emotions by our age-old cultural norms persists, and is perhaps even strengthened in reaction against the disintegration of authority taking place around us. The tension between Self and the world is ever growing, and sets our feelings in turmoil.

A good example of this is to be found in the case of that major deviation from the norm of sexuality known as 'homosexuality'. The interest in this here is not least because the very name is virtually new, deriving as it does from the medicalisation of our feelings little more than a hundred years ago. The activity itself, however, is immemorial and has been viewed as normal—institutionalised, even—in countless societies and cultures. Even in traditional Christian societies it was no more proscribed than were other pecadilloes—there was, after all, no name for it—and the interpretation of what the Bible (i.e., Leviticus) condemns was actually of sodomy, which could be as much a between-sex as a same-sex activity, and was in fact equally punished as such.

What is new to our times, then, is the way of diagnosing this condition: its clinical inherence in a given human-being. This supposed inherence only too well befits a world in which, for instance, a manager of a business cannot allow himself to consider what the dismissal of an employee might mean for that person's family: to have such feelings would destroy the rationale of management. Similarly, the heterosexual norm cannot allow of the healthiness of other kinds of feelings: these can only be pathological, as pertaining to a sick object regardless of its circumstances. This is not as much as to say (as is indeed said) that surely most people are actually, and from the womb, bisexual—just as managers might also have feelings; it is rather to call the very category of bisexuality into question. Nor is it necessary to contend (as it is indeed contended) that homosexuality is culturally determined, for in cultures wherein it has most unselfconsciously been practised there has been no name for it: i.e., it is not 'homosexuality'. It is to say, rather, that when in our ordinary discourse, our everyday language, we treat of the Self as monolithic, as if it were a real and substantial but isolated thing, we will find ourselves emotionally inhibited. Just as we are isolated from the world, we are distant from ourselves. 'Inner' and 'outer' worlds are in fact different perspectives of one and the same illusion of reality.

Of all our many forms of communication, indeed, it is words—not music, say, or painting, though these are not immune from the same influences—that most readily lend themselves to our atomistic worldview and which, ironically, have thereby made it most difficult for us to relate to one another. Literalism is a stultification of both feelings and imagination; it embodies the fallacy that words picture reality. St. Augustine's literalism, in conformity with his philosophy of language, by its unawareness of metaphor and allegory, destroyed the ancient myths. Conversely, Shakespeare, of course, and perhaps out of some profound disillusionment, a disillusionment with words themselves, understood the real currency of words and how easily it is debased:

> O, let me true in love, but truly write
> And then believe me, my love is as fair
> As any mother's child, though not so bright
> As those gold candles fixed in heaven's air.
>   Let them say more that like of hearsay well:
>   I will not praise that purpose not to sell.

Conversely, however, the language of touch is no respecter of persons, and those pathologically inured to the Self's isolation may shrink in horror from being touched. This does not necessarily refer to homosexuals—although there may of course be a certain pathology of isolation in the case of those thus characterised—but rather to the narcissism (i.e., egoism) so pervasive in our culture, and of which a loss of relationships is a prime feature. To communicate by touch is taboo amongst us—as it is also amongst other peoples with absolutist ideas of truth, such as the Indians with their caste system. (Of course, there can also be true or false touching. Whether a kiss is a genuine greeting or not will depend on the circumstances, as Christ knew all too well. But the taboo against our touching one another is fixated on the act itself, regardless of its context.) The rules of friendship, then, keep us at a distance from those who are tainted by one supposed pathology or another. And of course these rules are reinforced by the mechanism we commonly employ, of all the more vociferously condemning these 'pathologies' (as with 'queer-bashing') for fear that, behind our stereotyped masks, they might be discovered in ourselves. Conversely, the development of a gay culture would seem to be a tragic impoverishment of the lives, not only of those concerned, but of everyone else. 'Homosexuals', after all, have enriched our culture out of all proportion to their numbers. It is surely tragic that a 'gay' culture should now crave its own ghetto. It remains to be said, then, that when we allow the power of words to treat of our feelings in clinical detachment from the whole field of their meaning—from their environment, in fact— we impoverish ourselves emotionally.

Secondly, let us consider the words that cluster round the notion of economics and the economy. Economics as we know it today developed about a hundred years ago (another legacy from the end of the 19th century) from the establishment of Marginal Utility theory. It was this theory which allowed of the mathematisation of economic thought; and it is this, in turn, that has allowed of the abstraction of economic phenomena from all other social reality. Now, admittedly, Galileo said, 'The book of Nature is written in geometrical characters.' But does it follow that Nature's book is itself natural?

This is one of the great unresolved disputations in philosophy, and it is not going to be decided here as to whether the world must somehow conform—as, say, with $E=mc^2$—to mathematical design. Here it must be enough to point out that the Market, as the phenomenon upon which the notion of economics is based, is nothing but a stipulation. Its existence is simply what is needed to make Marginal Utility theory operable; the process is self-fulfilling.

The Market is in fact nothing but a metaphysical contrivance—a salient one of our age. Its principal component—sometimes crudely known as Economic Man—is a shameless reification; and the objects with which this homunculus interacts—the goods and services whose prices the Market determines by its Hidden Hand—are presented as real and isolated entities. No doubt a pound of meat is a pound of meat, is a pound of meat; but it does not exist in a vacuum. It gains its significance, its very recognition as a pound of meat, from all manner of different circumstances—as, for instance, part of a traditional English dinner, or from being part of a farmer's livelihood, as well as from a whole system of measurement—and from different people at different times. If the economist nevertheless wants to establish—by Marginal Utility analysis—the monetary value, the price, of this fictional object, well and good; but he will have achieved something of less than no significance. For he will have propagated something as fact that has no truth in it at all. In this light it may be easier to understand why, at about the same time this pseudo-science of economics was in gestation, Ruskin was moved to utter his dictum that 'the only wealth is life'.

Of course, this is not to say there are not markets—or at least, that these are not a useful figure of speech—but only that the great variety of them must make any abstraction of what is essentially economic about them impossible and meaningless. They are all variously compounded of political, legal and social factors, as well as economic; moreover, the utilitarian psychology upon which the notion of the Market is dependent is empirically simplistic in the extreme. To justify this last contention it is hardly necessary to do more than point to the degree of accuracy with which countless predictions of events have been made by economists over recent decades. It is not so amazing that these go on being made as that anyone pays attention to them. Clearly, they have us all bewitched. That they none the less continue to be valued is because they conform to the mental pattern, to the paradigm, that would exonerate us from all the complexity of considering things in context: that allows us to take matters out of context in order to perpetuate the illusion that things substantively exist, and that so therefore does the Self—for whom the homunculus of Economic Man is the surrogate.

We have already touched on the bizarre metaphysical exercise of cost-benefit analysis, which sustains the illusion (beyond all credibility) that the Market must somehow exist. Little different from this is the favoured antidote for our environmental problems: the 'polluter pays' principle. It is equally an illusion to suppose that payment can prevent pollution as such. It can only shift its incidence. We are all polluters all the time. Nothing can be produced without waste, less or more. If every activity paid for its own waste and nuisance—including, say, a charge for the atmosphere—there would in the first place be that much less activity to pay for it: indeed, virtually none at all. More to the point, however, as things are, though we all may suffer from each other's pollution, yet we also all benefit from the side effects of each other's activities. Rents are what reflect this fact; and, speaking technical economic theory, the factor of rent is present, not just in land-ownership, but in all economic transactions and in the values of their component elements. Logically, therefore, if we must be charged for pollution, we must also be compensated for the benefits we indirectly bestow. This, however, would be not just a *reductio ad absurdum*, but a recipe for economic disorder. Such disorder has in fact hitherto been avoided by the sheer discreteness, the particularity, of economic transactions. The desire to reify and circumscribe the Market (as also in the case of cost-benefit analysis) because of a compulsion to treat each transaction as if hypothetically it were fully accountable in itself, is an obfuscating and sterile digression from the actual environmental issue. If someone is creating a nuisance, then, let them be told to stop it. But the real damage the 'polluter pays' policy does is to make a travesty of the meaning of environment, making it something to be bought.

It is impossible, from these premises, not to go on by questioning the very notion of 'the economy'. Obviously it is as improbable that this exists as that economics, for all its fashionable mathematics, can ever be a separate science. Perhaps the best illustration of this is provided by the seminal (and intellectually beautiful) chapter on Buddhist Economics in Fritz Schumacher's *Small is Beautiful*. Schumacher, himself a highly qualified economist, out of his experience in Burma showed the idiosyncracity of a prime assumption of Western economics: that labour is but a factor of production. As such, we in the West treat work as a chore to be rewarded and compensated for. By contrast, the traditional Buddhist view sees work as the spiritual fulfillment of a person's life. This response is totally contrary to the prediction of western economic theory.

Now it is hardly a question of which set of values underlying these systems of value is in some sense right—though it would actually be very pertinent to ask who measures the measure. All that should be noted, rather, is that the West, in its need always to discover something 'out there', has imputed certain behaviour to people and called the result 'the economy': and that this is merely a metaphysic—and, should things go wrong with this 'economy', we will know who is ultimately to blame (i.e., the economists). What Schumacher is talking about, conversely, is actually life's inter-dependence: about labour as integral to life. (In this language game it is inconceivable that labour should be construed as an isolated factor of production.) In this light, he is in fact not talking about Buddhism, but rather about being local: about our being close enough unavoidably to connect with one another. We are therefore faced with two radically different vocabularies, conducive to two opposite structures of living. To exist in terms of the abstractions of 'the economy' is in fact to attempt to pursue life out of any context. Either such conceits should be comprehensively abandoned, or economics should invent pragmatic categories with which to function—new categories of entities with more meaning in these times—and forget about describing some mathematical never-never world. In any case, the language, and therefore laws, of economics (or any other 'social science') are derived, no matter how inferentially, from the language and rules in which society is constructed, and cannot therefore stand in a subject-object relation thereto. The more detached the economist is, the less he will understand. Economics is not physics... (and nor, perhaps, is physics!)

Thirdly, then, let us consider a concept concerning which there is an acknowledged and widespread malaise: education. Nor is that malaise surprising, for in a manner of speaking education is a microcosm, a mirror image, of our society at large. The confusion and apathy that has overtaken education only pre-figures the real world for which education is supposedly the preparation. Education, in fact, starkly exhibits the dualism on which our culture has its insecure foundations. This is represented, on the one hand, by Locke's notion of the child as a clean sheet waiting to be written upon by society and, on the other hand, by Rousseau's reaction against this (a hundred years later) of the child as a child—a person in its own right— and from which the whole practice of child-centred education has arisen. There, then, you have the age-old dualities: of the social and the personal, nurture and nature, the mechanistic and the Romantic, outer and inner, empirical and solipsistic, Caesar and God. And there is no possible resolution of them within the present paradigm.

In our own epoch—that is, since the seventeenth century—the dominant orthodoxy in education (inevitably, in view of the materialistic thrust of the Enlightenment) has been Lockean: of the child as a social atom, individual but conformist. To this the so-called Progressive movement has largely been only reactive, though child-centred education has by its radical nature enjoyed its fair share of intellectual influence. This influence was at its height in the heyday of the New Education Fellowship between the Wars; and, perhaps significantly, this coincided with the accelerated disintegration of communities, particularly of village life, after the Great War. This atmosphere of alienation was all too conducive to a withdrawal of the young into themselves, such as the Progressive movement offered. Ironically, however, it was largely the triumphant revolt of youth culture after the second war that made the Progressive movement in education redundant and, partly because of the associated drug practice of that culture, largely discredited. This, however, has not left the field to a victorious orthodoxy for, almost as if the departure of the opposition had deprived it of purpose, conventional education has simultaneously lost the confidence of the society it exists to serve. That society itself has begun fundamentally to change.

A clue to the reasons for this disharmony lies in the very notion of knowledge characteristic of the Enlightenment and epitomised in educational practice. This is demonstrated by the subject dominance of its classrooms—indeed, by the classroom itself. ('Subject', after all, is a curious word in this context. The child studies the subject, but it is the subject that rules the child; it is not the object of the child's study. The roles have been reversed. All word play apart, however, no doubt the subject in education is meant to be what is governed by knowledge; the kingdom of knowledge is thus divisible into specialisms. And the child, finally, is neither here nor there.) This academic view of knowledge has been all-powerful in both modes of education. True, it has caused most heart searching in the Progressive mode, in which the child is not the creature of adult priorities, and Dewey's precept of 'learning by doing' had a strong counter-influence in the inter-war heyday of the Progressive movement. This precept, however, was essentially contrived within the already artificial structure of a school. The school—any school—takes the child away from his environment. (One could even say, if provocatively, that schooling is an environmentally hostile concept.) The child is a sacrifice made to knowledge. Of its nature, this kind of knowledge is compartmentalised, and the classroom structure any school must adopt in the interests of control—and which constitutes the nucleus of power for each discipline—assures the child's isolation from his everyday world. (Of course, for some children the school offers a shelter from that world and this, rather than any educational practice, is perhaps the chief justification of schooling. But this point can't be pursued here.) Hence, in no matter how 'free' a school, the child is sure to fall victim to the exigent demands of the examination system that supplies all schools with some sort of a rationale. Moreover, this tyranny of specialisation leads by its own logic to an ever greater size of school and to ever more alienation of the child within it—in a foretaste of the world at large.

The idea of schooling, in fact, has become synonymous with education itself—though it is by no means sure that levels of literacy are any higher now than they were in the sixteenth century when the age of schooling began: and certainly not than when compulsory schooling began a little more than a hundred years ago. Be that as it may, the main characteristic of schooling, whether orthodox or Progressive, is actually just that it takes the child out of its everyday community. Yet the common complaint about the system today is that, for so much cost and effort, the child in school really learns very little. But is this surprising? The child, after all, has been taken out of its environment; and the primary motivation for any learning, surely, is appreciation of the meaning of what is being taught, which precisely depends on context. Thus a process of passing on the skills, knowledge and even wisdom of one generation to another has, over the centuries, been transposed from the everyday business of life into something with maybe the same name, 'education', but radically different in kind—and self-referring. Rather than perpetuating this fraud it would surely be better to call it simply 'instruction'.

To be fair to Locke and Rousseau, their notion of education had less to do with schools than with tutors. Rousseau, in fact, selected his pupil Emile from the aristocracy precisely because he considered his life therein was so artificial and so much further from Nature than the common people's. The latter were less in need of 'education'; such children, he thought, were already educated by life. However, the inexorable logic of the dualistic notion of knowledge has brought us to today's hopeless impasse. Education, however it may be tinkered with, cannot be changed by itself. Contrary to the idealism sometimes expressed for it, it will not change the world; rather, only the world can change it. In itself, education, that confection of subjects, has become a non-subject. And it will remain such until children cease to go to school in an urban neighbourhood or village but, rather, the village or neighbourhood, as well as the home, educates them.

This leads, fourth and last, to the saddest case of all: planning—and particularly urban, or land-use, planning. This is so sad because planning is a (would-be) profession dedicated, in our disaggregated society, to a wholeness of view, yet has found itself swimming against the tide of specialisation that is the element in which all the various professions must exist. In the result it has become a self-contradictory specialist in non-specialisation, and highly vulnerable as such. It is thus the opposite, virtually the mirror-image, of the cases previously considered. Their specialisation has isolated them from context, and hence from meaning; in the case of planning, meaning itself has been fixed in concrete—and hence rendered meaningless, for what is meaningful derives dynamically only from what is not meaningful. A whole that is fixed, complete, cannot bestow meaning upon its parts; it is spiritually dead.

The clue to the pall that has befallen planning, then, lies in the West's immemorial strain of idealistic thought. Planning has idealised the wholes with which, quite rightly, it is concerned: that is, the various forms of settlement, of cities, towns, villages and countryside. It is the dualism of the Western mind-set that has brought this idealisation about, just as much as it is responsible for the specialisms that follow from our reductionist method. Indeed, there is an inherent connection between idealism and our dualistic mentality. Given that the ideal depicts a reality beyond appearances, it is for the detached observer of those appearances to define the ideal. The ideal is thus perfect in itself, free of context, and nothing must mar its perfection. (It is, so to speak, reality without meaning.) Thus, with his dualistic mentality, the planner is detached from the city he idealises—and, in the fullness of the Western tradition, post-war planning in Britain was nothing if not idealistic.

The ideal city, moreover, presupposes the perfectibility of its inhabitants, they being part and parcel of its reality. Planning has thus lent itself to a kind of architectural determinism, of which the most notorious example has been the fashion for dense, high-rise development. This so-called 'urbanity' stemmed from an idealisation of the proletariat and took its inspiration from Vienna's Karl Marx Hof, and spread via Corbusier—he for whom a house was a machine to be lived in—to the Architects' Department, notoriously Marxist as it was, of the old London County Council. The infection even touched the post-war British new towns, to the great detriment of their public esteem, since these were only acceptable to the government of the day as little more than working-class housing estates, to which was added a dash of that equally idealistic folly of 'self-containment'. In brief, planning in Britain has been incorrigibly Utopian, and has proved a paradise only for the interfering bureaucracy without which all Utopias must be unattainable.

Our Utopians, however, remain in thrall to the quantitative: to the method that demands of reality that it should be measurable. Hence all forms of settlement must have their characteristic structures, and these are given by the functions suitable to them. The catchment area of a school will be one of these determinants—assuming that a school must be constituted of a certain number of subjects and classes, etc; hospitals, in the light of the current state of the medical art, will be another; sewage systems another; the fire service another, and so forth. Technical functions will determine community—if, indeed, there should be any community at the end of it: but at least these functions will be measurable. Planning has thus sought to fix in hierarchical aspic our various forms of settlement; it has tried, by its Key Settlement policy, to strangle villages that failed to meet its functional criteria (and merely turned them into havens for those seeking to avoid planning's kind of world), and it has failed to recognise the radically changing form of cities.

This last is well shown by the disaster that has overtaken London ever since the effective rejection of the Greater London Development Plan. This Plan, the major initiative of the newly created Greater London Council, was rightly savaged by its critics—all 28,207 of them—at the Inquiry into it in 1970. For many years the central Government, in various guises, then secretly consulted about what should be done and, eventually, ineptly decided to do nothing to disturb the sway of the thirty-two boroughs of which the city was politically (and quite arbitrarily) constituted. 'London', in other words, had no form. The abolition of its governing body—though neither the abolished, nor the abolitionists, apparently saw any connection between these events—could then only be a matter of time, and occurred some ten years later. London has since become notorious for the decline in its quality of life. It remains the only capital city without any kind of government.

At the root of this whole sorry state of affairs was a failure of the planners concerned to recognise that the very form of cities was changing: to recognise it, and to fight for it. All the influences of contemporary technology have, in fact, been conspiring to make of a city a many-centred, not a single-centred, urban form; and of course this has been happening *pari passu* with people's changing habits and demands—their demand for more than proportionately increasing house-room, for instance, as their incomes grow.

So it seems people do not want to be perfected by planning: not, at all events, if this means conforming to someone else's ideal. It took a small gas explosion that killed five people in an east London high-rise, Ronan Point, to bring down this whole intellectual pack of cards and burst the dam of people's resentment against planning. Does this mean, then, that market forces are actually the only sure guide to where and how we live: that a place can be nothing but their resultant? And is it infeasible to plan the forms of urban life as a whole?

It would be a sorry state of affairs if this were indeed the case. The driving persuasion of planning, after all, is that it holds the key, in this world of manifold alienations, to the determination of our identity. To be able to associate oneself with an identifiable place is to achieve one's own identity: it is, in a sense, to know oneself. But it is also to forget oneself, for it is to treat of community and the merging of selves therein. In other words, the true rationale of planning is non-dualism. Conversely, the more it persists with its dualistic methods, the more discredited it must become. These methods include the imposition of arbitrary and fixed distinctions, such as Green Belts, on existent agglomerations, and all the centralised decision-taking of the present system in its pursuit of perfection.

But there is no logical reason why we should not intentionally make the places where we live—though they might never become as we had expected them to be. The Zen of planning is, of course, an art still to be developed, and it is hard anyway to see how this could occur under the present hierarchical system of local government. Indeed, it might be unattainable without a fundamental change in the values of our culture. What is certain, however, is that the word 'planning' is so corrupted that to pursue any changes under its aegis would be doomed. Planning must return whence it came: to being a local social movement, with the issue of land values at its core.

These four conceptual areas, then—of our feelings, the economy, education and urban planning—are examples of where we are trapped by the very words we use and where changes in our vocabulary and its grammar must occur if ever we are to reach Byzantium, that mythological crossroads where all opposites dissolve. On one interpretation, after all, Wittgenstein's 'Philosophical Investigations', the work of his maturity, was nothing but a prolonged deconstruction of the substantive existence of the Self. His was the big exercise. For the rest of us there is remedial work enough to keep us busy for an indefinite future.

Chapter Nine

Right Livelihood

EACH OF US KNOWS that we shall die. In fact, we know it from very early on and, whatever we each may take our death to mean, this awareness imparts a special intensity to the idea of our life. The temptation to reify, to actualise, a transcendent Self is a product of this intensity. Whether or not this temptation is succumbed to, however, we each will surely have a conception of the wholeness of our life arising from our awareness of its finitude. This sense of wholeness calls for ostensible relationships between the manifold parts of one's life. Yet, at the same time, and whether or not any one of us achieves this sense of wholeness, actually to know a whole—any whole—is also to recognise its incompleteness. For 'The Tao that can be spoken of is not the Tao that is.'

The tension this implies expresses itself, then, in the would-be manufacture of a Self. The attraction of this attempt lies in our putting an end to the uncertainty accompanying the incompleteness of any whole governing our lives. Our fabricated Self, hopefully, will then be able to stand apart from the unruly world and in a position to order it; and to effect this (indeed, as the concomitant of being a Self, and of carrying this Self from place to place, from role to role) it treats of the world as composed of objects, of things. And to this temptation the West, as Nietzsche recognised, has comprehensively succumbed.

Of course, the consequences of this process with all its soteriological overtones, its hopes of salvation, has only been to intensify—albeit to repress—any fear of death that might (or might not) be innate in us, for awareness of death's inevitability is actually only enhanced by the stratagem of using the Self to order the world. Moreover, the more we cut the world up into manageable pieces, the harder it becomes to retain any sense of wholeness in our lives, and the more meaningless these must become. Nevertheless we strive to keep one step ahead of any such reckoning with the facts by continually expanding the area of our actions, seeking to complete the whole. Hence, the environmental phenomena with which we have become engaged are by now global in scale and significance. Understandably, therefore, we are sometimes enjoined to 'think globally, act locally!', and pictures of the earth taken from space serve to reinforce the message: the message that the micro- and the macroscopic must yet be reconciled, that meaning is after all as much local as global.

There is, however, a disturbing division developing here between thinking and acting. It is our thoughts that take us into the realms of metaphysics; all too easily they seduce us into conceiving of *the* Environment, and hence, in fact, into global prescriptions for our maladies. But to prescribe for the globe is a sure recipe for strife on a global scale. We can never catch up with our environment; it can never be snared in the net of thought.

Institutionally, the nation state has served to regulate the relationships that arise from our ever more fragmented lives and as, for instance, the relentlessly increasing proportion of public expenditure to national income testifies (for all the Canute-like protestations of governments), the pervasion of our lives by that institution inexorably grow. Nowadays the superstate is beginning to supplement the nation state, whilst simultaneously the greenhouse effect is bringing into question the very notion of national boundaries. But the superstate will no more be able to satisfy peoples' need for some meaning in their lives than can the nation state. Our restlessness is endemic. So absurdly remote, indeed, is government becoming from the everyday patterns of our lives—so meaningless, therefore—that arguably people will eventually be prepared once again to fashion communities of an intelligible size in which to lead their lives. Paradoxically, perhaps, the greenhouse effect could thus presage the break-up of the state.

Such an upshot, however, is hardly conceivable in mechanistic terms, simply by the exercise of some political edict. All the technology that has brought the state as we know it into being, and that sustains its existence, cannot be disinvented; yet that it should be is, one suspects, the necessary condition of any merely political suppression of the forces of centralisation. What would be required, therefore, for the break-up of modern states and their replacement by communities of a meaningful scale is a transforming change of values; and, in all realism, the only imaginable source of such a change is a catastrophe, or an impending catastrophe, comparable to nothing in Western history but the fall of Rome. (An Eastern equivalent could be the conversion of Asoka and his empire to Buddhism after the carnage of the Kalingas.) There is, of course, no guarantee that any catastrophe would halt us in the folly of our tracks; and the absence of any deep and widespread questioning of the events of 1991 in the Persian Gulf does not augur well for the possibility of change, since those events were but a portent of the coming challenge to our values. What is clear, however, is both that any impending catastrophe would be environmental in origin and that its avoidance would be dependent on our coming to understand the actual meaning of environment.

The fulcrum of that world whose values must fundamentally change if catastrophe is to be averted is the metaphysical Self. And the agent of this transformation is the notion of environment. Environment, it might be said, is that to which no Self, in its capacity as a detached observer, can belong. Environment annihilates Self, just as it negates the discrete objects that, for the metaphysical Self, compose the reality of the world. So far as language can convey our condition, then, the world is in fact composed, not of objects, of things, but of forms of life, of being. That is to say, therefore, of relationships: and not of relationships between things, but between relationships themselves in infinite regression, with no ultimate reference. An environment is hence a form of being in which observer and observed are dissolved.

Now the foregoing remarks might seem to be ontological: that is, in terms of the nature of reality. In truth, however, that would betoken too ambitious a purpose. All that is being explored here is the supercession of a certain cast of thought: the cast of dualistic thought that has dominated the last four centuries of Western culture and that was nurtured in the Christian era and the Classical age before it. Of course, this cast of thought has extraordinary credentials; its mastery of the material world is undoubted. But it is rapidly becoming clear that its understanding is only partial—inherently so— and, furthermore, that the world itself is not material. Our cast of dualistic thought is in fact flawed, and the flaws in its working are becoming plain for all to see—which is why environment is increasingly, if intuitively, being called in aid.

The situation this presents us with was foreseen in Buddhist philosophy more than two thousand years ago. That philosophy speaks of two kinds of truth: conventional truth and higher, or soteriological, truth. These two truths are not mutually exclusive, and higher truth cannot be reached except through conventional truth. Indeed, we obviously could not carry on our everyday life without recourse to conventional truth: that is, without dependence on the signs and grammar of the language we share with one another. But what is impermissible, given the demonstrable inability of conventional truth to penetrate beyond a certain level of phenomena—for instance, with regard to causation—is to step outside actual experience and to reason from metaphysical, a priori assumptions. Higher truth, rather, in this philosophy—and it is 'higher' only because it has a dimension of liberation, of health—demands resistance to this temptation and is a function, less of the language of thought, than of action (and this could include sitting meditation, or cooking a meal), but not excluding the action of language.

The same principle is to be found in Ecclesiasticus even though this was not thought fit for inclusion in the Bible proper. It speaks of the farmer ('whose discourse is of the stock of bulls'), of the smith, the artificer, the potter, and says of them:

All these shall put their trust in their hands,
And each becometh wise in his own work.
Without these shall not a city be inhabited
And men shall not sojurn nor walk up and down therein.
They shall not be sought for in the council of the people,
And in the assembly they shall not mount on high.
They shall not sit in the seat of the judge
And they shall not understand the covenant of judgement,
Neither shall they declare instruction and judgement,
And where parables are they shall not be found.

But they will maintain the fabric of the world,
And in the handywork of their craft is their prayer.

How, then, is everyday life to be resumed as a form of prayer, and to be plucked out of the bearpit in which it is now lived? The answer to this boils down to curbing the scope of the metaphysical Self. This Self is the product of hubris: of supposing itself, not just part of our necessary day-to-day conversation, but the detached and all-but God-like determinant of the laws governing the forces at work in the world. By now, the metaphysical Self has perhaps become the lord and master of society, if not yet totally of Nature. Intellectually, in fact, it is only the spreading environmental concern of these times that gives pause to our ruling rational materialists over the course on which they are set—although, to others, the spiritual emptiness of our culture and its rising drug practice, and all the alienation and its attendant violence, are already warning signs enough that this human demi-God is flawed.

It would be impossible to exaggerate the ramifications of this challenge by environment to the Self. Our whole everyday world, conducted as it is in terms of objects—products of our dualistic knowledge: knowledge of the world by the Self—must, in the light of that challenge, be acknowledged as but a mental construct. To restore health to the consumerist society this knowledge has generated will require a complete reconsideration of the Self: or, in common-or-garden terms, of our individualism. The condition of any such reconsideration is a restoration of meaning—that is, of connectedness—to the hustle and bustle of daily life: and of more meaning than is to be found by spending money for the sake of it (and just to alleviate boredom) in the shops. This betokens a life that, in institutional terms, speaks of a degree of local autonomy lost to Anglo-Saxon consciousness virtually since the Norman Conquest. But for that reason, and although it goes against the self-defeating, suicidal and inexorable current of centralisation, it is not inconceivable.

Fritz Schumacher, for example, used to talk of 'lifeboats'. By those he meant we would wait in vain—and he was criticised for this—for any transformation of society as a whole: we should, rather, launch small-scale experiments in alternative living. It was with this in mind that he initiated the appropriate technology movement, and began its application to the Third World. It is in the so-called First World, however, the seat of the misconceived and dangerous exercise of modern life, that as already said the application of his idea is urgent. And, indeed, it is happening here in an admirably pragmatic way, albeit with minimal help from established authority.

There is, then, the alternative health movement, with its centres for the practice of a variety of alternative medicines. There is the development of alternative energy, given new credibility by the pincer of our fears of the greenhouse effect and of atomic power. There is the alternative farming movement, with organic (and biodynamic) farming being made attractive by reason of the malaise in chemical agriculture. There is the stirring of an alternative education movement, with places like The Small School in the village of Hartland demonstrating that secondary education on a human scale and with less than forty children on the roll is, given the involvement of the village, entirely practicable. There is, one could say, alternative eating, in the form of vegetarianism: and alternative motoring with lead-free petrol. And so on: we are, in brief, changing our habits.

The foregoing examples all have in common a sense that there is a meaning to each of their activities over and beyond that of the activity itself. In one sphere of life, however, there is little comparable change in the prevalent and ruling assumption that knowledge of anything is self-justifying; the sphere where money holds sway and the question of possession dominates. There has not, in this sphere, been a move to the further dimension implicitly acknowledged in many 'alternative' activities. Indeed, where any such move has been attempted—whether totally, under communism, or partly, under socialism—it has been rejected with contumely by its subject peoples. Economic individualism is therefore again respectable.

This rejection of the public dimension, then, superficially would seem to argue against the wholeness associated with the alternative movement in general. But the wholeness of the state, in which public ownership is vested, is of a different order from the wholeness of an environment. It is, in fact, delusory; the 'wholeness' of the state is simply a function of physical size, of the scale on which the state operates. It is above all a wholeness of power; it ends, not where power loses its meaning, but where another power limits it and as the balance of power determines. The state is but the counterpart of the individual in the dialectic of politics—much as idealism is to solipsism; they are, as it were, of the same stuff. (The resolution of this dialectic in a stateless 'dictatorship of the proletariat' was never more than a callow delusion.) The scope for alternative ways of living in terms of the structure of the state—and hence of Green politics—is thus decidedly restricted. Possessiveness, after all, is the hardcore of all the structures based on dualistic thought, of which the mechanisms of the state are a prime example. It is the framework of that thought itself that is actually at issue, so far as the development of alternative ways of living are concerned.

There are cases of economic activity, however, other than state ownership, that more plausibly qualify for the status of one of Schumacher's 'lifeboats'. There are numerous co-operatives, both of producers and consumers, and some illustrious co-ownership enterprises—to say nothing of the many management buy-outs that of recent years have rescued from bankruptcy the alienated victims of financially-fixed industrial mergers. But perhaps the most imposing, yet at the same time disappointing, case of hopefully alternative economic life is the great Basque co-operative of Mondragon. With more than a score of enterprises, some of over a thousand owner-workers, and spreading over many square kilometres of countryside, Mondragon has been a potent agent of rural and national regeneration. Yet, for all that it was initiated by a Jesuit priest, it is irredeemably and virtually unashamedly materialistic in its values.

Maybe this only reflects how stupidly, in general, we organise our worldly affairs. Had it not been for the Jesuit priest, that is to say, Mondragon would have remained after the Spanish Civil War as depressed and disorganised as the rest of the area around it. No doubt, in fact, all our exploitation of the earth could be more intelligently—which is to say, ruthlessly—organised than it is. Nevertheless, in so far as that exploitation, however organised, is conducted in terms of some one criterion—that of profit, measured by money—each such organisation will be isolated thereby, a separate thing and unconditioned by any environment: to be validated, or not, only in those terms. Money, as the unit of measurement in terms of which our actions are usually validated, has a power which nullifies the launching of economic 'lifeboats'. It embodies, after all, the power of knowledge. Even if these 'lifeboats' should take the extreme form (though now quite discredited) of communes owning property in common, to establish such a commune—that is, one not insulated by some common faith—they must be exposed to the competition of conventional economic forms, and would assuredly succumb to them. For alternatives to work, then, money (like any other language) must be put in its place.

So are we condemned to endure the state as the regulating mechanism of our atomised world, and therefore, for all the profound changes taking place (as they are always taking place) in the chemistry of the human psyche, remain subject to structures conducive to monetary management? Must technology always rule the roost? There is little point in speculating on the bearing of impending catastrophe upon all our social structures. From the 'lifeboat' point of view, however, one is bound to note that the fall of Rome was an era when monastic life first became significant in the West. (Islam, of course, took a contrary way: that of militant monotheism and rejection of the monastic life. One cannot, indeed, ignore the attractions of resurgent fundamentalism in our own day and age.) But Christian monasticism is by no means the only possible model. Buddhist monasticism, for instance, differs from it in many ways, notably in that the nun or monk does not make a lifelong commitment to the monastery. In the world of today, then, another pattern of quasi-monastic life seems ripe for development: it could be described as of monks and nuns in the world. Examples are to be found in the activities of the Friends of the Western Buddhist Order in various parts of London, or of the Zen Center in San Francisco and other places in America.

The core of any such exercise, which goes far beyond the cooperative idea of a Mondragon, is the pursuit of what, in Buddhist terms, is known as Right Livelihood as part of a disciplined life in common. There is no need, however, for such establishments to be specifically Buddhist, nor indeed of any faith at all; nor need their participants be celibate. What is crucial, so far as any 'lifeboat' in the stormy seas of everyday economic life is concerned, is the notion of Right Livelihood, for this alone is invulnerable against the universalistic claims of money. Right Livelihood, then, means that in whatever way one gains one's living, one does not knowingly do harm in the process. And since one can never know with certainty whether what one does is harmful, one is circumspect in one's work. The mere maximisation of profit is thus unacceptable. Right Livelihood, in other words, means work that admits of environment. It is obviously unthinkable, for instance, that it would have condoned the irresponsible programmes of nuclear energy that many countries have embarked upon.

Right Livelihood, then, by leading towards a recognition of the mystery inherent in environment, is a necessary step in the deconstruction of the Self. This is reminiscent of Wittgenstein's notion of the Self (in The Tractatus) as the metaphysical subject that marks the limit of the world—not a part of it: 'I am my world.' Yet it might be argued that the same effect could be arrived at by, say, Japanese-style company cameraderie: a process of depersonalisation through the loss of individuality in mass identity. If this were so, no connection could be traced, surely, between environmental concern and the absence of Self; the Japanese, after all, are hardly noted for their environmental concern. (Their traditional concern for the purlieus of a private dwelling has yet to be extended to the city at large.) However, loss of Self in this way is by the path of nihilism. The Self as a nothing is a something; nihilism is an assertion of nothingness—and, being an assertion, is a something, something significant. Destruction of the Self by the Self—any act of self-immolation—is self-regarding, and its environment is the least of its concerns. Fascism, the epitome of nihilism, has no environmental content.

In brief, whether or not we call it Right Livelihood—and this may seem too foreign to be widely accepted (indeed, it may be too easily misunderstood as nothing but moralistic rigour)—the widespread launching of 'lifeboats' in the face of pending environmental catastrophe demands a new economic order. This implies, not so much a change in our values, but a change in the measure of value itself. Money alone can no longer be accepted as the sole criterion of economic activity; and should it be contended that economic activity is synonymous with what money can measure, then henceforth there can be no economic activity entertained in isolation from its responsibility to the world as a whole. How else, if we do not recognise this, shall we maintain the fabric of the world?

Chapter Ten

Whom the gods destroy,
they first make mad

THE TASK IS TO MAINTAIN the fabric of the world, not to re-make it. 'The sense of the world', said Wittgenstein, concluding his examination of logic, 'must be outside the world. In the world everything is as it is, and everything happens as it does happen... all that happens and is the case is accidental.' It is illusory to think we can alter the fabric of the world to any pattern of our liking; the values of any such exercise cannot but be flawed, built on sand. In the world 'no value exists—and if it did exist it would have no value.' It would, after all, take a shift of only a very few degrees in the temperature of the earth for all the bases of our morality to change. And, whether or not the earth's temperature should change, all our values are dependent upon each other in a continuous flux: none is autonomous, or fixed.

All of which may be true enough, yet nevertheless, in conventional truth, value does exist and we cannot but play language games with it. Why do we, then, busy as we are in the world, bother to make sense of the world when its sense lies outside it? Presumably it is because we talk, and hence perforce are civilised; and, being civilised, with our language we have fabricated a more-or-less sensible world. Yet this is not the world itself. Language is not a picture of the world; it is itself a part of the world, and we who use it cannot do so to escape the world or stand apart from it.

The austerity of Wittgenstein's stance is fully compatible with the notion of environment I wish to promote here. We cannot fabricate environment as such, and it is nonsensical to suppose we can. In trying to do so with one environment we only generate another. We can at most maintain an environment—though only by not striving to do so. It is, indeed, by striving to change it—to possess the very ground of our existence—that we have brought upon ourselves the environmental crisis so peculiar to our age.

Nevertheless, let it not be supposed that these propositions are a licence for fatalism, or an espousal of quietism. They are, rather, only a rejection of the claims of any criterion of value to a monopoly of the world. We are condemned to be active in the world, just as we are condemned to talk; but we cannot foretell the environmental effects of our activities, nor judge them. The pursuit of agriculture may produce a countryside, and of mining and industry a Black Country, and both may poison the rivers and the sky. But this is not to say that neither pursuit should be followed, or that both are beyond our prayers. We can only be mindful, far more circumspect than historically we have been, seduced by knowledge and surrendered to greed as we have been. The path of wisdom, surely, is the middle way between opposites—as, say, between asceticism and indulgence, or conservation and innovation—a pragmatic course that avoids the idealisation of any value. And similarly, between an idealisation of the past and of the future, the path of wisdom suggests action in this moment. (In each case, where the middle lies is of course a matter of cautious judgement. With genetic engineering, say, the perspective of responsible change must seem very different from that of the Channel Tunnel.)

Our current invocation of environment, then, is but a signal of our helplessness. It serves as a warning, no more, that our civilised values are at risk and that we are on a course of self-destruction. To misinterpret that warning by giving still more rein to our knowledge, to the mastery of the natural world, would be to make that destruction all the more probable. There is no green Utopia to be fabricated (any more so than any other kind). Why, then, should we be bothered with anything other than the self-regarding values of our civilised world? If we got that world's structures working mechanistically as well as could be wished, why should we worry about what anyway we cannot control? It is because, surely, we know that the justification of those values, if any, actually lies beyond that world. Our very respect for knowledge thus hoists us by our own petard.

This is as much as to accept, then, that we find ourselves in the midst of a mystery. Such an acceptance, however, is bound to be sustained by an enormous optimism derived from the fact that anything so marvellous as the world should exist at all, for it rests upon a conviction that, by being unafraid to accept the world as it is, our impulse to abuse our power of language will be constrained: and, in being constrained, that our temptation to subdue the world and possess it will at last be mastered. And should this come about and our bread, so to speak, be cast upon the waters, we might find ourselves at home again on the earth. Or, should our environment none the less still threaten our extinction—as, say, through collision of the earth with some great asteroid, such as probably wiped out the dinosaurs—at least we shall not have conspired in our own destruction.

So far, alas, our lease upon the mystery of the world has resulted only in a divorce of spirit from matter. Should we not be able to bring these together again, that lease will not be renewed. And if it is not, if we persist in the false pride of our power of speech, ours will be the first known case of a species' dominion over the earth being brought to an end because its masters had, at their own instance, made themselves pathologically mad.

Chapter Eleven

Coda

IF HUMANITY IS SINKING INTO MADNESS, it is perhaps of a purpose; for we live behind our stockade of language and, should our sense of reality fail us, chaos would overwhelm the defences of our sanity.

And, indeed, our defences *are* failing us. They are built on shifting sands; for language, far from truly representing the world, is forever changing as it is used. Poetry, catching meaning on the wing rather than explaining the world, is the only maker of any lasting worth; but Man proudly fabricates his habitation in prose, and so in self-delusion falls into this necessary madness: necessary, because to face the truth, that he may no longer be welcome on the earth, is too painful.

The mad, however, can hardly know they are mad—all the less when all are mad—any more than we can tell that the tightly-scripted parts we play in the world, the masks of conformity, are themselves the tragedy we are enacting. What is tragic is that we should be playing this tragedy. Only some token of grace, surely, some holy folly, might restore the sanity of humankind.

Environment, then, is this grace. It is the lifeline which presents itself, wherewith we might haul ourselves back to the ever-precarious shores of life on earth. Only... we must not mistake the meaning of this lifeline, or it will snap.